MODERN AMERICAN POETRY

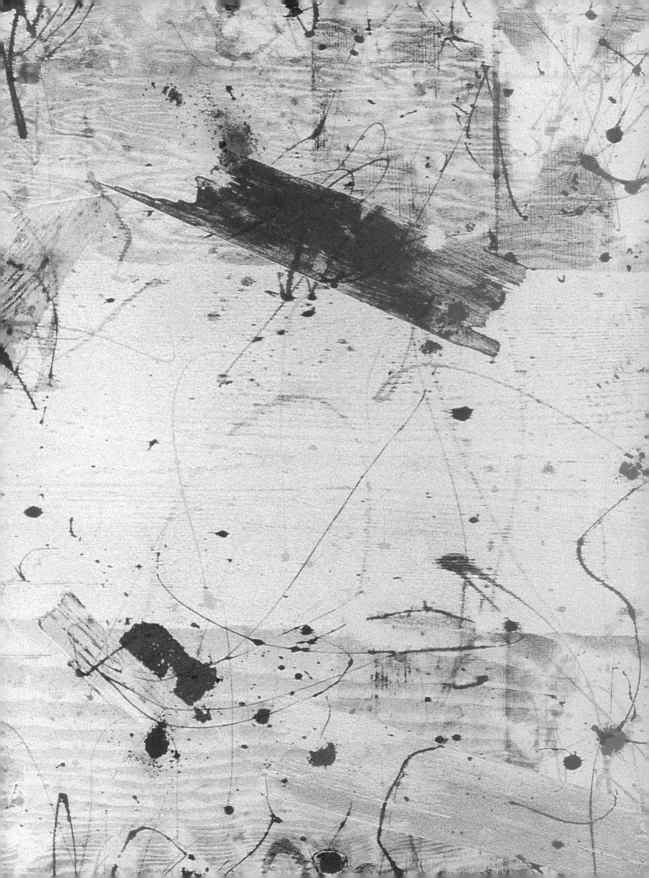

MODERN AMERICAN POETRY

SELECTED AND EDITED BY

JOSEPH COULSON

PETER TEMES

JIM BALDWIN

English department chair
Marin Academy

Published by the Great Books Foundation
A nonprofit educational organization

Published and distributed by

The Great Books Foundation
A nonprofit educational organization

35 East Wacker Drive, Suite 2300

Chicago, IL 60601-2298

www.greatbooks.org

ISBN 1-880323-88-5

First printing

9 8 7 6 5 4 3 2 1 0

Library of Congress Cataloging-in-Publication Data

Modern American poetry / edited by Joseph Coulson, Peter Temes, Jim Baldwin.
    p. cm.
    Summary: An anthology of poems for classroom discussion by American
poets from the mid-nineteenth century to the present day. Includes brief
biographies of the poets and guidelines for reading poetry.
    ISBN 1-880323-88-5
    1. American poetry—20th century. 2. American poetry—19th century.
[1. American poetry—Collections.] I. Coulson, Joseph. II. Temes, Peter
S., 1966– III. Baldwin, Jim, 1949–

PS613.M54 2002
811'.508—dc21
                                    2002066825

WHAT IS THE GREAT BOOKS FOUNDATION?

The Great Books Foundation is an independent, nonprofit educational organization whose mission is to help people learn how to think and share ideas. Toward this end, the Foundation offers workshops in shared inquiry discussion and publishes collections of classic and modern texts for both children and adults.

The Great Books Foundation was established in 1947 to promote liberal education for the general public. In 1962, the Foundation extended its mission to children with the introduction of Junior Great Books. Since its inception, the Foundation has helped thousands of people throughout the United States and in other countries begin their own discussion groups in schools, libraries, and community centers. Today, Foundation instructors conduct thousands of workshops each year, in which educators and parents learn to lead shared inquiry discussion.

WHAT RESOURCES ARE AVAILABLE TO SUPPORT MY PARTICIPATION IN SHARED INQUIRY?

The Great Books Foundation offers workshops in shared inquiry to help people get the most from discussion. Participants learn how to read actively, pose fruitful questions, and listen and respond to others effectively in discussion. All participants also practice leading a discussion and have an opportunity to reflect on the process with others. For more information about Great Books materials or workshops, call the Great Books Foundation at 1-800-222-5870 or visit our Web site at www.greatbooks.org.

A NOTE TO THE READER

Our intent in this collection is to suggest the range and vigor of modern American poets and their works, and to bring readers into a dialogue with the poems through reflection and discussion. Unlike other books published by the Great Books Foundation, the selections in *Modern American Poetry* are not followed by questions for discussion. Since poetry is rich in meaning and often compact, we felt the questions might overwhelm the poems on the page. As always, we extend an invitation to you, the reader, to create your own questions.

In the following pages, you'll find advice and models for developing questions based on close reading. The natural extension of personal dialogue with a poem is a larger conversation with members of a class or discussion group. We believe that the most useful discussions involve the method of shared inquiry, which is described in the section "About Shared Inquiry" (p. 21).

HOW TO READ A POEM

Reading poetry well is part attitude and part technique. Curiosity is a useful attitude, especially when it's free of preconceived ideas about what poetry is or should be. Effective technique directs your curiosity into asking questions, drawing you into a conversation with the poem.

In Great Books programs, the goal of careful reading is often to take up a question of meaning, an interpretive question that has more than one answer. Since the form of a poem is part of its meaning (for example, features such as repetition and rhyme may amplify or extend the meaning of a word or idea, adding emphasis, texture, or dimension), we believe that questions about form and technique, about the observable features of a poem, provide an effective point of entry for interpretation. To ask some of these questions, you'll need to develop a good ear for the musical qualities of language, particularly how sound and rhythm relate to meaning. This approach is one of many ways into a poem.

GETTING STARTED: PRIOR ASSUMPTIONS

Most readers make three false assumptions when addressing an unfamiliar poem. The first is assuming that they should understand what they encounter on the first reading, and if they don't, that something is wrong with them or with the poem. The second is assuming that the poem is a kind of code, that each detail corresponds to one, and only one, thing, and unless they can crack this code, they've missed the point. The third is assuming that the poem can mean anything readers want it to mean.

William Carlos Williams wrote a verse addressed to his wife in the poem "January Morning":

> All this—
> was for you, old woman.
> I wanted to write a poem
> that you would understand.
> For what good is it to me
> if you can't understand it?
> But you got to try hard—

Williams admits in these lines that poetry is often difficult. He also suggests that a poet depends on the effort of a reader; somehow, a reader must "complete" what the poet has begun.

This act of completion begins when you enter the imaginative play of a poem, bringing to it your experience and point of view. If a poem is "play" in the sense of a game or a sport, then you enjoy that it makes you work a little, that it makes you sweat a bit. Reading poetry is a challenge, but like so many other things, it takes practice, and your skills and insight improve as you progress.

Literature is, and has always been, the sharing of experience, the pooling of human understanding about living, loving, and dying. Successful poems welcome you in, revealing ideas that may not have been foremost in the writer's mind in the moment of composition. The best poetry has a magical quality—a sense of being more than the sum of its parts—and even when it's impossible to articulate this sense, this something more, the power of the poem is left undiminished.

Poems speak to us in many ways. Though their forms may not always be direct or narrative, keep in mind that a real person formed the moment of the poem, and it's wise to seek an understanding of that moment. Sometimes the job of the poem is to come closer to saying what cannot be said in other forms of writing, to suggest an experience, idea, or feeling that you can know but not entirely express in any direct or literal way. The techniques of word and line arrangement, sound and rhythm, add to—and in some cases, multiply—the meaning of words to go beyond the literal, giving you an impression of an idea or feeling, an experience that you can't quite put into words but that you know is real.

READING A POEM ALOUD

Before you get very far with a poem, you have to read it. In fact, you can learn quite a few things just by looking at it. The title may give you some image or association to start with. Looking at the poem's shape, you can see whether the lines are continuous or broken into groups (called *stanzas*), or how long the lines are, and so how dense, on a physical level, the poem is. You can also see whether it looks like the last poem you read by the same poet or even a poem by another poet. All of these are good qualities to notice, and they may lead you to a better understanding of the poem in the end.

But sooner or later, you're going to have to read the poem, word by word. To begin, read the poem aloud. Read it more than once. Listen to your voice, to the sounds the words make. Do you notice any special effects? Do any of the words rhyme? Is there a cluster of sounds that seem the same or similar? Is there a section of the poem that seems to have a rhythm that's distinct from the rest of the poem? Don't worry about why the poem might use these effects. The first step is to hear what's going on. If you find your own voice distracting, have a friend read the poem to you.

That said, it can still be uncomfortable to read aloud or to make more than one pass through a poem. Some of this attitude comes from the misconception that we should understand a poem after we first read it, while some stems from sheer embarrassment. Where could I possibly go to read aloud? What if my friends hear me?

THE LINE

What determines where a line stops in poetry? There is, of course, more than one answer to this question. Lines are often determined by meaning, sound and rhythm, breath, or typography. Poets may use several of these elements at the same time. Some poems are metrical in a strict sense (in "A Note on Meter," p. 491, you'll find a discussion of meter and other forms of rhythmic organization in lines of poetry). But what if the lines aren't metrical? What if the lines are irregular?

The relationship between meaning, sound, and movement intended by the poet is sometimes hard to recognize, but there is an interplay between the grammar of a line, the breath of a line, and the way lines are broken out in the poem—this is called *lineation*. For example, lines that end with punctuation, called *end-stopped lines*, are fairly simple. In that case, the punctuation and the lineation, and perhaps even breathing, coincide to make the reading familiar and even predictable. But lines that are not end-stopped present different challenges for readers because they either end with an incomplete phrase or sentence or they break before the first punctuation mark is reached. The most natural approach is to pay strict attention to the grammar and punctuation. Reading to the end of a phrase or sentence, even if it carries over one or several lines, is the best way to retain the grammatical sense of a poem.

But lineation introduces another variable that some poets use to their advantage. Robert Creeley is perhaps best known for breaking lines across expected grammatical pauses. This technique often introduces secondary meaning, sometimes in ironic contrast with the actual meaning of the complete grammatical phrase. Consider these lines from Creeley's poem "The Language":

> Locate *I*
> *love you* some-
> where in
>
> teeth and
> eyes, bite
> it but

Reading the lines as written, as opposed to their grammatical relationship, yields some strange meanings. "Locate *I*" seems to indicate a search for identity, and indeed it may, but the next line, which continues with *"love you* some-," seems to make a diminishing statement about a relationship. On its own, "eyes bite" is very disturbing.

Hearing Creeley read his poems can often be disquieting, because he pauses at the end of each line, and these pauses create a kind of tension or counterpoint in relation to the poem's sentence structure. His halting, hesitant, breathless style is immediately recognizable, and it presents writers with new ideas about meaning, purely through lineation. But many poets who break lines disregarding grammatical units do so only for visual irony, something that may be lost in performance. Among metrical, free verse, and even experimental poets of today, there are those who do not interrupt grammatical sense when reading a poem aloud as much as they interrupt it in the poem's typography. What to do as a reader? Try a variety of methods. It's fun to "Creeleyize" any poem, just to hear what the lineation is doing. But if the results seem to detract from the poem's impact, in terms of its imagery or concept, drop the literal treatment of line breaks and read for grammar or visual image. Reading a poem several ways allows you to see further into the poem simply through repetition.

With poets who use techniques drawn from music—particularly jazz, such as Michael S. Harper or Yusef Komunyakaa—or poets like Walt Whitman who employ unusually long lines, there may be another guiding principle: breath. Some poets think of their words as music flowing from a horn; they think of phrases the way a saxophonist might. Poems composed in this way have varied line lengths, but they have a musicality in their lineation and a naturalness to their performance. They may have a recognizable sense of measure, an equivalent duration between lines, or, for the sake of contrast, one rhythmic pattern or duration that gives way to successive variations.

For some poems, visual impact may also be important. In "shaped poetry," as well as many other types of writing that are meant to be seen as a painting might be seen, the line is determined by its placement in space. Some visually oriented poets present real challenges in that the course of the poem may not be entirely clear. Visual choices presented by the poet may be confusing. Sometimes the arrangements of words on a page are intended to represent different voices in a dialogue, or even a more complex discourse on a subject. Overlapping and layering might be the poet's intent, which no single voice can achieve. It's best to be aware that poems with multiple voices or focuses exist and, again, looking for the inherent rules that determine the shape of the poem is the best approach.

Remember that the use of these techniques, in any combination, pushes the words of the poem beyond their literal meanings. If you find more in a poem than the words alone convey, then something larger is at work, making the poem more than the sum of its parts.

Starting the Conversation

We mentioned earlier that encountering a difficult poem is like a game or sport—say, rock climbing—that makes you work a bit. The idea of finding handholds and footholds and ascending one bit at a time is apt. But some climbs are easier than others; some are very easy. You may enjoy an easy climb for a while, but you may also find that you want a bigger challenge. Reading poetry works the same way, and, fortunately, poets leave trails to help you look for the way "up" a poem. You'll have to do some work, hard work in some cases, but most of the time, the trails are there for you to discover.

At the Great Books Foundation, we believe that the best way to discover and learn about a poem is through shared inquiry discussion. Although your first experience of the poem may be private and personal, we think talking about the poem is a natural and important next step. Beginning with a focus question about the poem, the discussion addresses various possible answers to the question, reshaping and clarifying it along the way. The discussion should remain grounded in the text as much as possible. Responses that move away from what is written into personal anecdotes or tangential leaps should be gently urged back into analyzing the text. The basis for shared inquiry is close reading. Good readers "dirty the text" with notes in the margins. They make the inquiry their own. We encourage you to write your own notes in this book.

TALKING BACK TO A POEM

It would be convenient if there were a short list of universal questions, ones that could be used anytime with any poem. In the absence of such a list, here are a few general questions that you *might* ask when approaching a poem for the first time.

Who is the speaker?
What circumstances gave rise to the poem?
What situation is presented?
Who or what is the audience?
What is the tone?
What form, if any, does the poem take?
How is form related to content?
Is sound an important, active element of the poem?
Does the poem spring from an identifiable historical moment?
Does the poem speak from a specific culture?
Does the poem have its own vernacular?
Does the poem use imagery to achieve a particular effect?
What kind of figurative language, if any, does the poem use?
If the poem is a question, what is the answer?
If the poem is an answer, what is the question?
What does the title suggest?
Does the poem use unusual words or use words in an unusual way?

You can fall back on these questions as needed, but experience suggests that since each poem is unique, such questions will not go the necessary distance. In many instances, knowing who the speaker is may not yield any useful information. There may be no identifiable occasion that inspired the poem. But poems do offer clues about where to start. Asking questions about the observable features of a poem will help you find a way in.

We'll now bring inquiry to bear on two very different poems: "The Red Wheelbarrow," by William Carlos Williams, and "Diving into the Wreck," by Adrienne Rich. Each poem presents its own challenges. The handwritten notes represent questions that occurred to the reader, questions that can be used to investigate the poem's form and meaning. Different readers will ask different questions about the poems.

THE RED WHEELBARROW

so much depends   *What depends?*

upon

a red wheel   *Why isn't there any punctuation?*

barrow

glazed with rain   *The long and short lines look choppy.*

water

beside the white   *Nothing could possibly be as simple as this. Could it?*

chickens

This poem can be infuriating because it appears so guileless and simplistic. The problem is that you can't take anything for granted, not even simplicity.

What are the first things you notice about the poem? Begin with what you know, or what you think you know. First, the poem is arranged in fairly consistent lines. The four units of the poem look somewhat alike. There isn't any punctuation either. What was the poet's intention? Was the shape an accident of the poet's descriptive style? Was the lack of punctuation an oversight? Was the poet being careless or lazy? Was is that he just couldn't think of any better words? Why is this poem so well known, so respected, so well liked?

Denise Levertov, in "Some Notes on Organic Form," says "there is a form in all things (and in our experience) which the poet can discover and reveal." But how does a poet make this discovery? One way is to pay close attention to the sound and movement of the first words or lines that begin the act of writing, in which the object, mood, and experience that give rise to the poem will often be expressed through tone and rhythm. Do the words work together to create euphony, dissonance, or something in between? What are the weights and inherent durations of words and lines? The poet who is sensitive to this emerging form can give it full play as writing continues.

Robert Creeley, in "Notes Apropos 'Free Verse,'" uses the analogy of driving to explain his approach to organic form in writing: "The road, as it were, is creating itself momently in one's attention to it, there, visibly, in front of the car." He implies that there may be more around the bend or beyond the horizon; but, like drivers, poets can only arrive at that possibility through careful attention to what is immediately apparent. Poets must follow the words, like the road, as they come.

When you read a poem, you must be both observant and patient. Look at the words and the lines as they emerge. What do you recognize? What looks or sounds interesting? Wait a little. Welcome surprises. As more of the poem reveals itself, you may find an exhilarating momentum, recognizable patterns, or a merging of form and content that will carry you along.

So how does "The Red Wheelbarrow" unfold? A helpful exercise is to try to continue writing the poem yourself. Double the length, either by repeating the theme or by adding a new riff about the images of the first eight lines. This is an experiential way of discovering what is noticeable about the poem. You will likely write in two-line stanzas, or *couplets*. Most of the second lines of the couplets will consist of a single word. Many will have those words be nouns, or two-syllable words. Aha! So you have already begun to notice how the poem is put together.

This brings us to the poem's statement, its meaning. Many poems, especially nonnarrative poems, are difficult—if not impossible—to paraphrase, especially after a first reading or a first listen. And expecting to find a meaning that's obvious is often frustrating, as it may be here. Why does so much depend? So much what?

Artists often say that a work of art is about itself and something else. In this way, a poem can be an *ars poetica,* a statement by the poet about poetry, about his or her beliefs about what poetry is and about what it does. Asking how this poem might be an *ars poetica* is a great way to further understand both the poem and Williams as a poet. What does the poem demonstrate about poetry? Well, certainly the features of style and form come up again. But the statement that the poem makes, the credo it represents, is right there, too. Another way to ask the question might be, What does this poem value? Common things, clearly. The only objects in the poem are ordinary, enduring, and somehow essential. The scene is rural, perhaps a farm. The chickens are not symbolic; they are white chickens that exist beside equally plain things of the world: a utilitarian barrow that is not exalted, but left out in the rain. And not an apocalyptic rain but a slow drizzle. Why does Williams choose this image, this scene? Why does so much of the poem depend on things so ordinary? Do these concrete things suggest a larger, more abstract idea?

It should be clear at this point that inquiry into earlier questions about form and technique have yielded larger questions of interpretation. So let's return for a moment to a question of form. All that's left from the list of first impressions is the lack of punctuation. How would the lack of stops anywhere in the poem reinforce the idea that ordinary things are of great importance? What does grammar accomplish in any text? For one thing, it helps determine beginnings and endings, and for another, it works with conjunctions to represent relationships among things, time, and ideas in the text. But in this poem, there is none of that. Why? Without the interruptions of commas and periods, the words flow together. They are not discrete parts but one whole unit, differentiated only by the space between couplet or stanza. But the pairing of lines seems to create a unity as well: four equal parts. So the "scene" is integrated further by the lack of any hierarchy imposed by punctuation. The grammar remains, of course.

So the stanzas stand on the page as separate, but the lack of punctuation connects them. Thereby, a tension is created, an independence that somehow is connected. This is beginning to sound like the statement the poem is making: "so much" depends on these humble things. The great and small, apparently distinct objects (and the stanzas) are nonetheless interconnected. Form and content are joined in a dance to create meaning, as is so often the case in art.

Here is a poem, Adrienne Rich's "Diving into the Wreck," that is quite different from Williams's. While "The Red Wheelbarrow," although speaking to a larger subject, is short, literal, and dependent on imagery, Rich's poem is long, metaphorical, and also dependent on imagery. It presents different challenges and opens different doorways to experience. And "Diving into the Wreck," no less than "The Red Wheelbarrow," provides a window into the soul of the poet and into the nature of inquiry itself.

DIVING INTO THE WRECK

First having read the book of myths,
and loaded the camera,
and checked the edge of the knife-blade,
I put on
the body-armor of black rubber
the absurd flippers
the grave and awkward mask.
I am having to do this
not like Cousteau with his
assiduous team
aboard the sun-flooded schooner
but here alone.

what use are a book, a camera, and a knife to the diver?

There is a ladder.
The ladder is always there   *Why is the ladder*
hanging innocently   *always there?*
close to the side of the schooner.
We know what it is for,
we who have used it.
Otherwise
it's a piece of maritime floss
some sundry equipment.

I go down.
Rung after rung and still
the oxygen immerses me
the blue light
the clear atoms
of our human air.
I go down.   *Why do the*
My flippers cripple me,   *flippers cripple*
I crawl like an insect down the ladder *the diver?*
and there is no one
to tell me when the ocean
will begin.

First the air is blue and then
it is bluer and then green and then
black I am blacking out and yet   *What is happening*
my mask is powerful   *to the diver?*
it pumps my blood with power
the sea is another story
the sea is not a question of power
I have to learn alone
to turn my body without force
in the deep element.

14

And now: it is easy to forget
what I came for
among so many who have always
lived here
swaying their crenellated fans

> *What does crenellated mean?*

between the reefs
and besides
you breathe differently down here.

> *How and why does the diver breathe differently "down here"?*

I came to explore the wreck.
The words are purposes.
The words are maps.

> *How are words "purposes" and "maps"?*

I came to see the damage that was done
and the treasures that prevail.
I stroke the beam of my lamp
slowly along the flank
of something more permanent
than fish or weed

the thing I came for:
the wreck and not the story of the wreck
the thing itself and not the myth
the drowned face always staring

> *What is the difference between the wreck itself and the story of the wreck?*

toward the sun
the evidence of damage
worn by salt and sway into this threadbare beauty
the ribs of the disaster
curving their assertion
among the tentative haunters.

This is the place.
And I am here, the mermaid whose dark hair
streams black, the merman in his armored body
We circle silently
about the wreck
we dive into the hold.
I am she: I am he   *How can the diver be both?*

whose drowned face sleeps with open eyes
whose breasts still bear the stress
whose silver, copper, vermeil cargo lies
obscurely inside barrels
half-wedged and left to rot
we are the half-destroyed instruments   *In what way is*
that once held to a course   *the diver like the*
the water-eaten log   *wreck?*
the fouled compass

We are, I am, you are
by cowardice or courage
the one who find our way
back to this scene
carrying a knife, a camera
a book of myths
in which   *Why are the names not*
our names do not appear.   *in the book?*

1972

What do you notice first? What about the title? Where Williams's title identified an object, which was then named in the poem as well, Rich titles her poem after an action. The title is dynamic, and so there's a good chance the poem will be too. What more does the title suggest? Along with mentioning Jacques Cousteau, the title connects an action with exploration and investigation. So now, what wreck? Is the poem an account of an adventure from some vacation cruise? How might you decide that the poem is a metaphor? The first line announces some kind of departure from the literal with "the book of myths." Archeologists may be informed by books of legend, but if Rich were referring to any such literal source, she would be more specific. There isn't a single "book of myths." Second, unlike Cousteau, this diver will go it alone. Given the cumbersome equipment and the importance of safety, this sounds unrealistic.

So, if this poem is an extended metaphor, the next questions might concern the necessary preparations for the dive: the book, the camera, and the knife. What implications are present in these details? (This is a good general question.) The book suggests a history or previous stories about the "wreck," whatever it may be. The camera is a device for recording what is factually present, as opposed to what is purportedly present. And the knife suggests danger. The last two are consistent with an actual wreck.

Something else you may notice reading through the poem several times is that the idea of being alone changes as the poem continues, but this change takes place in a rather unusual way. You might ask, therefore, what significance there is in the movement from "alone" to "among so many who have always lived here" to "We circle silently / about the wreck" to "I am she: I am he / whose drowned face sleeps," and finally, "We are, I am, you are / ... the one who find our way / back...."? By the end, the identity of the narrator is both one and many. Why?

Usually, the movement from one to many would indicate that the speaker found a community, belonging, or companionship. But here, the shifting identity, which moves between one and many, and between male and female, isn't immediately comfortable. Whether, as Rich says, "by cowardice or courage," the exploration and discovery of new territory is still in a kind of uncertainty about identity, if not an identity crisis. At the end, the names (plural) of these explorers, "do not appear" in the book of myths, indicating both a past disenfranchisement of some sort and a future change, created through the exploration of the wreck.

So, by asking questions without reference to biographical information, it's possible to isolate two significant thematic elements of Rich's poem, one of exploration and claiming territory, the other of transformation of identity, perhaps including gender identity. When looking at the date at the bottom of the poem, it's tempting to ask how the poem connects to the more general history of the early 1970s, particularly to the women's movement and the cultural change of that era.

However, it is not necessary to determine more specifically what the wreck might be. There is no need to reduce the poem to feminine identity and gender stereotypes, although clearly that element is present. There also is no need to limit the poem to a piece about artistic self-discovery. The poem doesn't have an "answer," and the result of personal inquiry or shared inquiry should only be to narrow and clarify some likely thematic possibilities, not to eliminate all conflict and ambiguity.

Clearly there are further elements of the poem to question as well, such as the relationship between lineation (or form in general) and content. The opposition—or perhaps *balance* is the better word—of "damage" and "treasures that prevail" is another intriguing issue. In a lengthier discussion, these and other elements could be explored.

TEXT AND CONTEXT

Some people say that a poem is always an independent work of art and that readers can make full sense of it without having to use any source outside the poem itself. Others say that no text exists in a vacuum. However, the truth lies somewhere in between. Most poems are open to interpretation without the aid of historical context or knowledge about the author's life. In fact, it's often best to approach a poem without the kind of preconceived ideas that can accompany this kind of information. Other poems, however, overtly political poems in particular, will benefit from some knowledge of the poet's life and times. The amount of information needed to clearly understand depends on you and your encounter with the poem. It's possible, of course, even for someone with a deep background in poetry to be unaware of certain associations or implications in a poem. This is because poems are made of words that accumulate new meanings over time.

Consider this situation, a true story, of a poet who found a "text" at the San Mateo coast in northern California. As she scrambled over rocks behind the beach, near the artichoke fields that separate the shore from the coast highway, she found a large smear of graffiti painted on the rocks, proclaiming *"La Raza,"* a Chicano political slogan meaning "the struggle." She sat down and wrote a poem. Why? her poem asked. I understand, she wrote, why someone would write *La Raza* on the side of a building, or on public transport. There it would be seen and would shout its protest from the very foundations of the oppressive system. But why here, in nature, in beauty, so far from that political arena. Couldn't you leave the coast unspoiled? Then, one evening while reading the poem in Berkeley she got her answer. A man came up to her and asked her, "Do you want to know?" "I beg your pardon," she said. "Those fields," the man went on, "were where Chicanos had been virtually enslaved, beaten, and forced to live in squalor for decades." The landscape was not innocent of political struggle. The text was not out of place.

EMBRACE AMBIGUITY

Here's a tricky issue: the task is to grasp, to connect, to understand. But such a task is to some degree impossible, and most people want clarity. At the end of class, at the end of the day, we want revelation, a glimpse of the skyline through the lifting fog. Aesthetically, this is understandable. Some magic, some satisfaction, some "Ahhh!" is one of the rewards of any reading, and particularly the reading of poetry. But a poem that reveals itself completely in one or two readings will, over time, seem less of a poem than one that constantly reveals subtle recesses and previously unrecognized meanings.

Here's a useful analogy. A life partner, a husband, a wife—these are people with whom we hope to constantly renew our love. Despite the routine, the drone of familiarity, the daily preparation of meals and doing of dishes, the conversations we've had before, we hope to find a sense of discovery, of surprise. The same is true of poems. The most magical and wonderful poems are ever renewing themselves, which is to say they remain ever mysterious.

Too often we resist ambiguity. Perhaps our lives are changing so fast that we long for stability somewhere, and because most of the reading we do is for instruction or information, we prefer it without shades of gray. We want it to be predictable and easy to digest. And so difficult poetry is the ultimate torment.

Some literary critics would link this as well to the power of seeing, to the relationship between subject and object. We wish the poem to be object so we can possess it through our "seeing" its internal workings. When it won't allow us to "objectify" it, we feel powerless.

Torment, powerlessness—these are the desired ends? Well, no. The issue is our reaction, how we shape our thoughts through words. We have to give up our material attitude, which makes us want to possess the poem. Maybe we've bought the book, but we don't own the poem. We have to cultivate a new mindset, a new practice of enjoying the inconclusive.

Embracing ambiguity is a much harder task for some than for others. Nothing scares some people like the idea (even the *idea*) of improvisation as a writing or analytical tool. Some actors hate being without a script; the same is true of some musicians. Ask even some excellent players to improvise and they start to sweat. Of course, actors and musicians will say that there is mystery in what they do with a script or a score, and it would be pointless to disagree. The point, after all, is that text is mysterious. Playing the same character night after night, an actor discovers something in the lines, some empathy for the character, that he or she had never felt before. Playing or listening to a song for the hundredth time—if it is a great song—will yield new interpretation and discovery. So it is with great poetry.

ABOUT SHARED INQUIRY

Shared inquiry is the effort to achieve a more thorough understanding of a text by discussing questions, responses, and insights with others. For both the leader and the participants, careful listening is essential. The leader guides the discussion by asking questions about specific ideas and problems of meaning in the text, but does not seek to impose his or her own interpretation on the group.

During a shared inquiry discussion, group members consider a number of possible ideas and weigh the evidence for each. Ideas that are entertained and then refined or abandoned are not thought of as mistakes, but as valuable parts of the thinking process. Group members gain experience in communicating complex ideas and in supporting, testing, and expanding their thoughts. Everyone in the group contributes to the discussion, and while participants may disagree with each other, they treat each other's ideas respectfully.

This process of communal discovery is vital to developing an understanding of important texts and ideas, rather than merely cataloging knowledge about them. By reading and thinking together about important works, you and the other members of your group are joining a great conversation that extends across the centuries.

Guidelines for Leading and Participating in Discussion

Over the past fifty years, the Great Books Foundation has developed guidelines that distill the experience of many discussion groups, with participants of all ages. We have found that when groups follow the procedures outlined below, discussions are most focused and fruitful.

1. **Read the selection before participating in the discussion.** This ensures that all participants are equally prepared to talk about the ideas in the work, and helps prevent talk that would distract the group from its purpose.

2. **Support your ideas with evidence from the text.** This keeps the discussion focused on understanding the selection and enables the group to weigh textual support for different answers and to choose intelligently among them.

3. **Discuss the ideas in the selection, and try to understand them fully before exploring issues that go beyond the selection.** Reflecting on a range of ideas and the evidence to support them makes the exploration of related issues more productive.

4. **Listen to others and respond to them directly.** Shared inquiry is about the give-and-take of ideas, a willingness to listen to others and to talk to them respectfully. Directing your comments and questions to other group members, not always to the leader, will make the discussion livelier and more dynamic.

5. **Expect the leader to ask questions, rather than answer them.** The leader is a kind of chief learner, whose role is to keep discussion effective and interesting by listening and asking questions. The leader's goal is to help the participants develop their own ideas, with everyone (the leader included) gaining a new understanding in the process. When participants hang back and wait for the leader to suggest answers, discussion falters.

HOW TO MAKE DISCUSSIONS MORE EFFECTIVE

- **Ask questions when something is unclear.** Simply asking someone to explain what he or she means by a particular word, or to repeat a comment, can give everyone in the group time to think about the idea in depth.

- **Ask for evidence.** Asking "What in the text gave you that idea?" helps everyone better understand the reasoning behind an answer, and it allows the group to consider which ideas have the best support.

- **Ask for agreement and disagreement.** "Does your idea agree with hers, or is it different?" Questions of this kind help the group understand how ideas are related or distinct.

- **Reflect on discussion afterward.** Sharing comments about how the discussion went and ideas for improvement can make each discussion better than the last.

ROOM ARRANGEMENT AND GROUP SIZE

Ideally, everyone in a discussion should be able to see and hear everyone else. When it isn't possible to arrange the seating in a circle or horseshoe, encourage group members to look at the person talking, acknowledging one another and not just the leader.

In general, shared inquiry discussion is most effective in groups of ten to twenty participants. If a group is much bigger than twenty, it is important to ensure that everyone has a chance to speak. This can be accomplished either by dividing the group in half for discussion or by setting aside time at the end of discussion to go around the room and give each person a chance to make a brief final comment.

WALT WHITMAN

1819–1892

Walt Whitman wrote poetry that most in his day considered scandalous. Open form, sexual content, an eye for the common and the ugly as well as the extraordinary and the beautiful, sympathy for the poor and the dispossessed—these are just some of the characteristics that made Whitman's poetry radical and unique. He self-published the first edition of *Leaves of Grass* in 1855 and wrote anonymous reviews that praised the author. He sent a copy to Ralph Waldo Emerson, who immediately recognized Whitman's talent. In 1862, as the Civil War escalated, Whitman nursed soldiers in Washington hospitals. His writing in this period, including his elegy for Abraham Lincoln, "When Lilacs Last in the Dooryard Bloom'd," constitutes a poetic history of the war. An innovator in diction, line, rhythm, and subject matter, Whitman stands as the father of modern American poetry.

The greatest poet does not moralize or make applications of morals . . . he knows the soul.

1

I celebrate myself, and sing myself,
And what I assume you shall assume,
For every atom belonging to me as good belongs to you.

I loafe and invite my soul,
I lean and loafe at my ease observing a spear of summer grass.
My tongue, every atom of my blood, form'd from this soil, this air,
Born here of parents born here from parents the same, and their
    parents the same,
I, now thirty-seven years old in perfect health begin,
Hoping to cease not till death.

Creeds and schools in abeyance,
Retiring back a while suffced at what they are, but never forgotten,
I harbor for good or bad, I permit to speak at every hazard,
Nature without check with original energy.

2

Houses and rooms are full of perfumes, the shelves are crowded
    with perfumes,
I breathe the fragrance myself and know it and like it,
The distillation would intoxicate me also, but I shall not let it.

The atmosphere is not a perfume, it has no taste of the distillation,
    it is odorless,
It is for my mouth forever, I am in love with it,
I will go to the bank by the wood and become undisguised and naked,
I am mad for it to be in contact with me.

The smoke of my own breath,

Echoes, ripples, buzz'd whispers, love-root, silk-thread, crotch and vine,

My respiration and inspiration, the beating of my heart, the passing
of blood and air through my lungs,

The sniff of green leaves and dry leaves, and of the shore and
dark-color'd sea-rocks, and of hay in the barn,

25   The sound of the belch'd words of my voice loos'd to the eddies
of the wind,

A few light kisses, a few embraces, a reaching around of arms,

The play of shine and shade on the trees as the supple boughs wag,

The delight alone or in the rush of the streets, or along the fields
and hill-sides,

The feeling of health, the full-noon trill, the song of me rising from
bed and meeting the sun.

30   Have you reckon'd a thousand acres much? have you reckon'd
the earth much?

Have you practis'd so long to learn to read?

Have you felt so proud to get at the meaning of poems?

Stop this day and night with me and you shall possess the origin
of all poems,

You shall possess the good of the earth and sun, (there are millions
of suns left,)

35   You shall no longer take things at second or third hand, nor look
through the eyes of the dead, nor feed on the spectres in books,

You shall not look through my eyes either, nor take things from me,

You shall listen to all sides and filter them from your self.

I have heard what the talkers were talking, the talk of the beginning
    and the end,
But I do not talk of the beginning or the end.

40 There was never any more inception than there is now,
Nor any more youth or age than there is now,
And will never be any more perfection than there is now,
Nor any more heaven or hell than there is now.

Urge and urge and urge,
45 Always the procreant urge of the world.

Out of the dimness opposite equals advance, always substance and
    increase, always sex,
Always a knit of identity, always distinction, always a breed of life.

To elaborate is no avail, learn'd and unlearn'd feel that it is so.

Sure as the most certain sure, plumb in the uprights, well entretied,
    braced in the beams,
50 Stout as a horse, affectionate, haughty, electrical,
I and this mystery here we stand.

Clear and sweet is my soul, and clear and sweet is all that is not
    my soul.

Lack one lacks both, and the unseen is proved by the seen,
Till that becomes unseen and receives proof in its turn.

55 Showing the best and dividing it from the worst age vexes age,
Knowing the perfect fitness and equanimity of things, while they
    discuss I am silent, and go bathe and admire myself.

Welcome is every organ and attribute of me, and of any man
    hearty and clean,
Not an inch nor a particle of an inch is vile, and none shall be
    less familiar than the rest.

I am satisfied—I see, dance, laugh, sing;
60 As the hugging and loving bed-fellow sleeps at my side through
    the night, and withdraws at the peep of the day with
    stealthy tread,
Leaving me baskets cover'd with white towels swelling the house
    with their plenty,
Shall I postpone my acceptation and realization and scream at my eyes,
That they turn from gazing after and down the road,
And forthwith cipher and show me to a cent,
Exactly the value of one and exactly the value of two, and which
    is ahead?

Passing stranger! you do not know how longingly I look upon you,
You must be he I was seeking, or she I was seeking, (it comes to
    me as of a dream,)
I have somewhere surely lived a life of joy with you,
All is recall'd as we flit by each other, fluid, affectionate, chaste,
    matured,
5 You grew up with me, were a boy with me or a girl with me,
I ate with you and slept with you, your body has become not yours
    only nor left my body mine only,
You give me the pleasure of your eyes, face, flesh, as we pass, you
    take of my beard, breast, hands, in return,
I am not to speak to you, I am to think of you when I sit alone
    or wake at night alone,
I am to wait, I do not doubt I am to meet you again,
I am to see to it that I do not lose you.

We two boys together clinging,
One the other never leaving,
Up and down the roads going, North and South excursions making,
Power enjoying, elbows stretching, fingers clutching,
Arm'd and fearless, eating, drinking, sleeping, loving,
No law less than ourselves owning, sailing, soldiering, thieving,
    threatening,
Misers, menials, priests alarming, air breathing, water drinking,
    on the turf or the sea-beach dancing,
Cities wrenching, ease scorning, statutes mocking, feebleness chasing,
Fulfilling our foray.

1

O take my hand Walt Whitman!
Such gliding wonders! such sights and sounds!
Such join'd unended links, each hook'd to the next,
Each answering all, each sharing the earth with all.

5   What widens within you Walt Whitman?
What waves and soils exuding?
What climes? what persons and cities are here?
Who are the infants, some playing, some slumbering?
Who are the girls? who are the married women?
10   Who are the groups of old men going slowly with their arms about
      each other's necks?
What rivers are these? what forests and fruits are these?
What are the mountains call'd that rise so high in the mists?
What myriads of dwellings are they fill'd with dwellers?

2

Within me latitude widens, longitude lengthens,
15   Asia, Africa, Europe, are to the east—America is provided for
      in the west,
Banding the bulge of the earth winds the hot equator,
Curiously north and south turn the axis-ends,
Within me is the longest day, the sun wheels in slanting rings, it
      does not set for months,
Stretch'd in due time within me the midnight sun just rises above
      the horizon and sinks again,
20   Within me zones, seas, cataracts, forests, volcanoes, groups,
Malaysia, Polynesia, and the great West Indian islands.

3

What do you hear Walt Whitman?

I hear the workman singing and the farmer's wife singing,
I hear in the distance the sounds of children and of animals early
    in the day,
I hear emulous shouts of Australians pursuing the wild horse,
I hear the Spanish dance with castanets in the chestnut shade, to
    the rebeck and guitar,
I hear continual echoes from the Thames,
I hear fierce French liberty songs,
I hear of the Italian boat-sculler the musical recitative of old poems,
I hear the locusts in Syria as they strike the grain and grass with
    the showers of their terrible clouds,
I hear the Coptic refrain toward sundown, pensively falling on the
    breast of the black venerable vast mother the Nile,
I hear the chirp of the Mexican muleteer, and the bells of the mule,
I hear the Arab muezzin calling from the top of the mosque,
I hear the Christian priests at the altars of their churches, I hear
    the responsive base and soprano,
I hear the cry of the Cossack, and the sailor's voice putting to sea
    at Okotsk,
I hear the wheeze of the slave-coffle as the slaves march on, as
    the husky gangs pass on by twos and threes, fasten'd together
    with wrist-chains and ankle-chains,
I hear the Hebrew reading his records and psalms,
I hear the rhythmic myths of the Greeks, and the strong legends
    of the Romans,
I hear the tale of the divine life and bloody death of the beautiful
    God the Christ,

40   I hear the Hindoo teaching his favorite pupil the loves, wars,
        adages, transmitted safely to this day from poets who wrote
        three thousand years ago.

4

What do you see Walt Whitman?
Who are they you salute, and that one after another salute you?

I see a great round wonder rolling through space,
I see diminute farms, hamlets, ruins, graveyards, jails, factories,
        palaces, hovels, huts of barbarians, tents of nomads upon
        the surface,
45   I see the shaded part on one side where the sleepers are sleeping,
        and the sunlit part on the other side,
I see the curious rapid change of the light and shade,
I see distant lands, as real and near to the inhabitants of them as
        my land is to me.

I see plenteous waters,
I see mountain peaks, I see the sierras of Andes where they range,
50   I see plainly the Himalayas, Chian Shahs, Altays, Ghauts,
I see the giant pinnacles of Elbruz, Kazbek, Bazardjusi,
I see the Styrian Alps, and the Karnac Alps,
I see the Pyrenees, Balks, Carpathians, and to the north the
        Dofrafields, and off at sea mount Hecla,
I see Vesuvius and Etna, the mountains of the Moon, and the
        Red mountains of Madagascar,
55   I see the Lybian, Arabian, and Asiatic deserts,
I see huge dreadful Arctic and Antarctic icebergs,

I see the superior oceans and the inferior ones, the Atlantic and Pacific,
     the sea of Mexico, the Brazilian sea, and the sea of Peru,
The waters of Hindustan, the China sea, and the gulf of Guinea,
The Japan waters, the beautiful bay of Nagasaki land-lock'd in its
     mountains,
60   The spread of the Baltic, Caspian, Bothnia, the British shores, and
     the bay of Biscay,
The clear-sunn'd Mediterranean, and from one to another of its islands,
The White sea, and the sea around Greenland.

I behold the mariners of the world,
Some are in storms, some in the night with the watch on the look-out,
65   Some drifting helplessly, some with contagious diseases.

I behold the sail and steamships of the world, some in clusters in
     port, some on their voyages,
Some double the cape of Storms, some cape Verde, others capes
     Guardafui, Bon, or Bajadore,
Others Dondra head, others pass the straits of Sunda, others cape
     Lopatka, others Behring's straits,
Others cape Horn, others sail the gulf of Mexico or along Cuba
     or Hayti, others Hudson's bay or Baffin's bay,
70   Others pass the straits of Dover, others enter the Wash, others the
     firth of Solway, others round cape Clear, others the Land's End,
Others traverse the Zuyder Zee or the Scheld,
Others as comers and goers at Gibraltar or the Dardanelles,
Others sternly push their way through the northern winter-packs,
Others descend or ascend the Obi or the Lena,
75   Others the Niger or the Congo, others the Indus, the Burampooter
     and Cambodia,

Others wait steam'd up ready to start in the ports of Australia,
Wait at Liverpool, Glasgow, Dublin, Marseilles, Lisbon, Naples,
    Hamburg, Bremen, Bordeaux, the Hague, Copenhagen,
Wait at Valparaiso, Rio Janeiro, Panama.

5

I see the tracks of the railroads of the earth,
80   I see them in Great Britain, I see them in Europe,
I see them in Asia and in Africa.

I see the electric telegraphs of the earth,
I see the filaments of the news of the wars, deaths, losses, gains,
    passions, of my race.

I see the long river-stripes of the earth,
85   I see the Amazon and the Paraguay,
I see the four great rivers of China, the Amour, the Yellow River,
    the Yiang-tse, and the Pearl,
I see where the Seine flows, and where the Danube, the Loire, the
    Rhone, and the Guadalquiver flow,
I see the windings of the Volga, the Dnieper, the Oder,
I see the Tuscan going down the Arno, and the Venetian along the Po,
I see the Greek seaman sailing out of Egina bay.

There was a child went forth every day,
And the first object he look'd upon, that object he became,
And that object became part of him for the day or a certain part
　　of the day,
Or for many years or stretching cycles of years.

5　The early lilacs became part of this child,
And grass and white and red morning-glories, and white and red
　　clover, and the song of the phoebe-bird,
And the Third-month lambs and the sow's pink-faint litter, and
　　the mare's foal and the cow's calf,
And the noisy brood of the barnyard or by the mire of the pond-side,
And the fish suspending themselves so curiously below there, and
　　the beautiful curious liquid,
10　And the water-plants with their graceful flat heads, all became part
　　of him.

The field-sprouts of Fourth-month and Fifth-month became part of him,
Winter-grain sprouts and those of the light-yellow corn, and the
　　esculent roots of the garden,
And the apple-trees cover'd with blossoms and the fruit afterward,
　　and wood-berries, and the commonest weeds by the road,
And the old drunkard staggering home from the outhouse of the
　　tavern whence he had lately risen,
15　And the schoolmistress that pass'd on her way to the school,
And the friendly boys that pass'd, and the quarrelsome boys,
And the tidy and fresh-cheek'd girls, and the barefoot negro boy and girl,
And all the changes of city and country wherever he went.

His own parents, he that had father'd him and she that had conceiv'd
　　him in her womb and birth'd him,
20　They gave this child more of themselves than that,
They gave him afterward every day, they became part of him.

　　　　　　　　　　　　　　　　　　　　　　　　　　　　　WALT WHITMAN

The mother at home quietly placing the dishes on the supper-table,

The mother with mild words, clean her cap and gown, a wholesome
odor falling off her person and clothes as she walks by,

The father, strong, self-sufficient, manly, mean, anger'd, unjust,

25   The blow, the quick loud word, the tight bargain, the crafty lure,

The family usages, the language, the company, the furniture, the
yearning and swelling heart,

Affection that will not be gainsay'd, the sense of what is real, the
thought if after all it should prove unreal,

The doubts of day-time and the doubts of night-time, the curious
whether and how,

Whether that which appears so is so, or is it all flashes and specks?

30   Men and women crowding fast in the streets, if they are not
flashes and specks what are they?

The streets themselves and the façades of houses, and goods in
the windows,

Vehicles, teams, the heavy-plank'd wharves, the huge crossing at
the ferries,

The village on the highland seen from afar at sunset, the river
between,

Shadows, aureola and mist, the light falling on roofs and gables of
white or brown two miles off,

35   The schooner near by sleepily dropping down the tide, the little
boat slack-tow'd astern,

The hurrying tumbling waves, quick-broken crests, slapping,

The strata of color'd clouds, the long bar of maroon-tint away
solitary by itself, the spread of purity it lies motionless in,

The horizon's edge, the flying sea-crow, the fragrance of salt marsh
and shore mud,

These became part of that child who went forth every day, and
who now goes, and will always go forth every day.

Thee for my recitative,
Thee in the driving storm even as now, the snow, the winter-day declining,
Thee in thy panoply, thy measur'd dual throbbing and thy beat convulsive,
Thy black cylindric body, golden brass and silvery steel,
5 Thy ponderous side-bars, parallel and connecting rods, gyrating,
   shuttling at thy sides,
Thy metrical, now swelling pant and roar, now tapering in the distance,
Thy great protruding head-light fix'd in front,
Thy long, pale, floating vapor-pennants, tinged with delicate purple,
The dense and murky clouds out-belching from thy smoke-stack,
10 Thy knitted frame, thy springs and valves, the tremulous twinkle
   of thy wheels,
Thy train of cars behind, obedient, merrily following,
Through gale or calm, now swift, now slack, yet steadily careering;
Type of the modern—emblem of motion and power—pulse of
   the continent,
For once come serve the Muse and merge in verse, even as here I see thee,
15 With storm and buffeting gusts of wind and falling snow,
By day thy warning ringing bell to sound its notes,
By night thy silent signal lamps to swing.

Fierce-throated beauty!
Roll through my chant with all thy lawless music, thy swinging
   lamps at night,
20 Thy madly-whistled laughter, echoing, rumbling like an earthquake,
   rousing all,
Law of thyself complete, thine own track firmly holding,
(No sweetness debonair of tearful harp or glib piano thine,)
Thy trills of shrieks by rocks and hills return'd,
Launch'd o'er the prairies wide, across the lakes,
To the free skies unpent and glad and strong.

EMILY DICKINSON

1830–1886

A prolific writer, Emily Dickinson is known to have composed nearly eighteen hundred poems, only a few of which were published in her lifetime. Dickinson led an intense intellectual life, pursuing friendships with several of the prominent men in her community, but she rarely left her family home. Many of her relationships were conducted through letters, often filled with her poetry. She often did not adhere to, and sometimes intentionally strayed from, conventions of spelling, capitalization, and punctuation. Today Dickinson is thought of as a great original, and along with Whitman—whose book she would not read because she had been told he was "disgraceful"—she is recognized as one of the founders of modern American poetry.

If I read a book [and] it makes my whole body so cold no fire can ever warm me, I know that is poetry. If I feel physically as if the top of my head were taken off, I know that is poetry.

I taste a liquor never brewed -
From Tankards scooped in Pearl -
Not all the Frankfort Berries
Yield such an Alcohol!

5   Inebriate of air - am I -
And Debauchee of Dew -
Reeling - thro' endless summer days -
From inns of molten Blue -

When "Landlords" turn the drunken Bee
10   Out of the Foxglove's door -
When Butterflies - renounce their "drams" -
I shall but drink the more!

Till Seraphs swing their snowy Hats -
And Saints - to windows run -
15   To see the little Tippler
Leaning against the - Sun!

I'm Nobody! Who are you?
Are you - Nobody - too?
Then there's a pair of us!
Don't tell! they'd advertise - you know!

5   How dreary - to be - Somebody!
How public - like a Frog -
To tell one's name - the livelong June -
To an admiring Bog!

[I FELT A FUNERAL, IN MY BRAIN]

I felt a Funeral, in my Brain,
And Mourners to and fro
Kept treading - treading - till it seemed
That Sense was breaking through -

5   And when they all were seated,
A Service, like a Drum -
Kept beating - beating - till I thought
My mind was going numb -

And then I heard them lift a Box
10   And creak across my Soul
With those same Boots of Lead, again,
Then Space - began to toll,

As all the Heavens were a Bell,
And Being, but an Ear,
15   And I, and Silence, some strange Race
Wrecked, solitary, here -

And then a Plank in Reason, broke,
And I dropped down, and down -
And hit a World, at every plunge,
And Finished knowing - then -

This World is not conclusion.
A Species stands beyond -
Invisible, as Music -
But positive, as Sound -
5   It beckons, and it baffles -
Philosophy, dont know -
And through a Riddle, at the last -
Sagacity, must go -
To guess it, puzzles scholars -
10   To gain it, Men have borne
Contempt of Generations
And Crucifixion, shown -
Faith slips - and laughs, and rallies -
Blushes, if any see -
15   Plucks at a twig of Evidence -
And asks a Vane, the way -
Much Gesture, from the Pulpit -
Strong Hallelujahs roll -
Narcotics cannot still the Tooth
That nibbles at the soul -

The Soul selects her own Society -
Then - shuts the Door -
To her divine Majority -
Present no more -

5   Unmoved - she notes the Chariots - pausing -
At her low Gate -
Unmoved - an Emperor be kneeling
Opon her Mat -

I've known her - from an ample nation -
10   Choose One -
Then - close the Valves of her attention -
Like Stone -

I died for Beauty - but was scarce
Adjusted in the Tomb
When One who died for Truth, was lain
In an adjoining Room -

5   He questioned softly "Why I failed"?
"For Beauty", I replied -
"And I - for Truth - Themself are One -
We Bretheren, are", He said -

And so, as Kinsmen, met a Night -
10   We talked between the Rooms -
Until the Moss had reached our lips -
And covered up - Our names -

I heard a Fly buzz - when I died -
The Stillness in the Room
Was like the Stillness in the Air -
Between the Heaves of Storm -

5   The Eyes around - had wrung them dry -
And Breaths were gathering firm
For that last Onset - when the King
Be witnessed - in the Room -

I willed my Keepsakes - Signed away
10   What portion of me be
Assignable - and then it was
There interposed a Fly -

With Blue - uncertain - stumbling Buzz -
Between the light - and me -
15   And then the Windows failed - and then
I could not see to see -

Undue Significance a starving man attaches
To Food -
Far off - He sighs - and therefore - Hopeless -
And therefore - Good -

5   Partaken - it relieves - indeed -
But proves us
That Spices fly
In the Receipt - It was the Distance -
Was Savory -

[PERCEPTION OF AN OBJECT COSTS]

Perception of an Object costs
Precise the Object's loss -
Perception in itself a Gain
Replying to it's price -

5   The Object absolute, is nought -
Perception sets it fair
And then upbraids a Perfectness
That situates so far -

EDGAR LEE MASTERS

1868–1950

Edgar Lee Masters's *Spoon River Anthology* (1915) ranks as one of the most popular and financially successful books of American poetry ever published. Spending his boyhood in rural Illinois, near the Spoon River, Masters was intimately familiar with the Midwestern life portrayed in his work. A successful lawyer, Masters wrote several volumes of prose, including political tracts, essays, and fiction, but nothing he wrote before or after *Spoon River* achieved comparable popularity or critical acclaim. Masters used poetry as a vehicle for his strong liberal views. He saw himself as a Midwestern populist and was disturbed by the prevailing influence of the East Coast establishment in American poetry. In 1946, the Academy of American Poets awarded Masters a fellowship for distinguished poetic achievement.

*I have many times in my life crushed down my heart
for the sake of poetry.*

"DUTCH" WELDY

After I got religion and steadied down
They gave me a job in the canning works,
And every morning I had to fill
The tank in the yard with gasoline,
5   That fed the blow-fires in the sheds
To heat the soldering irons.
And I mounted a rickety ladder to do it,
Carrying buckets full of the stuff.
One morning, as I stood there pouring,
10   The air grew still and seemed to heave,
And I shot up as the tank exploded,
And down I came with both legs broken,
And my eyes burned crisp as a couple of eggs.
For someone left a blow-fire going,
15   And something sucked the flame in the tank.
The Circuit Judge said whoever did it
Was a fellow-servant of mine, and so
Old Rhodes' son didn't have to pay me.
And I sat on the witness stand as blind
20   As Jack the Fiddler, saying over and over,
"I didn't know him at all."

Seeds in a dry pod, tick, tick, tick,
Tick, tick, tick, like mites in a quarrel—
Faint iambics that the full breeze wakens—
But the pine tree makes a symphony thereof.
5   Triolets, villanelles, rondels, rondeaus,
Ballades by the score with the same old thought:
The snows and the roses of yesterday are vanished;
And what is love but a rose that fades?
Life all around me here in the village:
10   Tragedy, comedy, valor and truth,
Courage, constancy, heroism, failure—
All in the loom, and oh what patterns!
Woodlands, meadows, streams and rivers—
Blind to all of it all my life long.
15   Triolets, villanelles, rondels, rondeaus,
Seeds in a dry pod, tick, tick, tick,
Tick, tick, tick, what little iambics,
While Homer and Whitman roared in the pines?

ANNE RUTLEDGE

Out of me unworthy and unknown
The vibrations of deathless music;
"With malice toward none, with charity for all."
Out of me the forgiveness of millions toward millions,
And the beneficent face of a nation
Shining with justice and truth.
I am Anne Rutledge who sleep beneath these weeds,
Beloved in life of Abraham Lincoln,
Wedded to him, not through union,
But through separation.
Bloom forever, O Republic,
From the dust of my bosom!

I went to the dances at Chandlerville,
And played snap-out at Winchester.
One time we changed partners,
Driving home in the moonlight of middle June,
And then I found Davis.
We were married and lived together for seventy years,
Enjoying, working, raising the twelve children,
Eight of whom we lost
Ere I had reached the age of sixty.
I spun, I wove, I kept the house, I nursed the sick,
I made the garden, and for holiday
Rambled over the fields where sang the larks,
And by Spoon River gathering many a shell,
And many a flower and medicinal weed—
Shouting to the wooded hills, singing to the green valleys.
At ninety-six I had lived enough, that is all,
And passed to a sweet repose.
What is this I hear of sorrow and weariness,
Anger, discontent and drooping hopes?
Degenerate sons and daughters,
Life is too strong for you—
It takes life to love Life.

EDWIN ARLINGTON ROBINSON

1869–1935

Like Edgar Lee Masters, Edwin Arlington Robinson spent his childhood in a small town that would become the setting for many of his poems. Robinson's experiences with poverty and his antimaterialist views shaped much of his poetry. Robinson struggled for years to gain recognition as a writer. Eventually he attracted the attention of President Theodore Roosevelt, who arranged a position for Robinson in the New York Customs House, one with few duties, which allowed ample time for writing. By 1919, Robinson was at last enjoying critical and popular success, spurring the publication of his *Collected Poems*, for which he won the first of three Pulitzer Prizes.

I realized finally… that I was doomed, or elected,
or sentenced for life, to the writing of poetry….
I kept the grisly secret to myself.

Go to the western gate, Luke Havergal,
There where the vines cling crimson on the wall,
And in the twilight wait for what will come.
The leaves will whisper there of her, and some,
Like flying words, will strike you as they fall;
But go, and if you listen she will call.
Go to the western gate, Luke Havergal—
Luke Havergal.

No, there is not a dawn in eastern skies
To rift the fiery night that's in your eyes;
But there, where western glooms are gathering,
The dark will end the dark, if anything:
God slays Himself with every leaf that flies,
And hell is more than half of paradise.
No, there is not a dawn in eastern skies—
In eastern skies.

Out of a grave I come to tell you this,
Out of a grave I come to quench the kiss
That flames upon your forehead with a glow
That blinds you to the way that you must go.
Yes, there is yet one way to where she is,
Bitter, but one that faith may never miss.
Out of a grave I come to tell you this—
To tell you this.

Whenever Richard Cory went down town,
We people on the pavement looked at him:
He was a gentleman from sole to crown,
Clean favored, and imperially slim.

5   And he was always quietly arrayed,
And he was always human when he talked;
But still he fluttered pulses when he said,
"Good-morning," and he glittered when he walked.

And he was rich—yes, richer than a king—
10   And admirably schooled in every grace:
In fine, we thought that he was everything
To make us wish that we were in his place.

So on we worked, and waited for the light,
And went without the meat, and cursed the bread;
15   And Richard Cory, one calm summer night,
Went home and put a bullet through his head.

MINIVER CHEEVY

Miniver Cheevy, child of scorn,
    Grew lean while he assailed the seasons;
He wept that he was ever born,
    And he had reasons.

5 Miniver loved the days of old
    When swords were bright and steeds were prancing;
The vision of a warrior bold
    Would set him dancing.

Miniver sighed for what was not,
10   And dreamed, and rested from his labors;
He dreamed of Thebes and Camelot,
    And Priam's neighbors.

Miniver mourned the ripe renown
    That made so many a name so fragrant;
15 He mourned Romance, now on the town,
    And Art, a vagrant.

Miniver loved the Medici,
    Albeit he had never seen one;
He would have sinned incessantly
20   Could he have been one.

Miniver cursed the commonplace
    And eyed a khaki suit with loathing;
He missed the mediaeval grace
    Of iron clothing.

25 Miniver scorned the gold he sought,
    But sore annoyed was he without it;
Miniver thought, and thought, and thought,
    And thought about it.

Miniver Cheevy, born too late,
30   Scratched his head and kept on thinking;
Miniver coughed, and called it fate,
    And kept on drinking.

THE DARK HILLS

Dark hills at evening in the west,
Where sunset hovers like a sound
Of golden horns that sang to rest
Old bones of warriors under ground,
5   Far now from all the bannered ways
Where flash the legions of the sun,
You fade—as if the last of days
Were fading, and all wars were done.

Old Eben Flood, climbing alone one night
Over the hill between the town below
And the forsaken upland hermitage
That held as much as he should ever know
On earth again of home, paused warily.
The road was his with not a native near;
And Eben, having leisure, said aloud,
For no man else in Tilbury Town to hear:

"Well, Mr. Flood, we have the harvest moon
Again, and we may not have many more;
The bird is on the wing, the poet says,
And you and I have said it here before.
Drink to the bird." He raised up to the light
The jug that he had gone so far to fill,
And answered huskily: "Well, Mr. Flood,
Since you propose it, I believe I will."

Alone, as if enduring to the end
A valiant armor of scarred hopes outworn,
He stood there in the middle of the road
Like Roland's ghost winding a silent horn.
Below him, in the town among the trees,
Where friends of other days had honored him,
A phantom salutation of the dead
Rang thinly till old Eben's eyes were dim.

Then, as a mother lays her sleeping child
Down tenderly, fearing it may awake,
He set the jug down slowly at his feet
With trembling care, knowing that most things break;
And only when assured that on firm earth
It stood, as the uncertain lives of men
Assuredly did not, he paced away,
And with his hand extended paused again:

"Well, Mr. Flood, we have not met like this
In a long time; and many a change has come
35 To both of us, I fear, since last it was
We had a drop together. Welcome home!"
Convivially returning with himself,
Again he raised the jug up to the light;
And with an acquiescent quaver said:
40 "Well, Mr. Flood, if you insist, I might.

"Only a very little, Mr. Flood—
For auld lang syne. No more, sir; that will do."
So, for the time, apparently it did,
And Eben evidently thought so too;
45 For soon amid the silver loneliness
Of night he lifted up his voice and sang,
Secure, with only two moons listening,
Until the whole harmonious landscape rang—

"For auld lang syne." The weary throat gave out,
50 The last word wavered, and the song was done.
He raised again the jug regretfully
And shook his head, and was again alone.
There was not much that was ahead of him,
And there was nothing in the town below—
55 Where strangers would have shut the many doors
That many friends had opened long ago.

Much as he left it when he went from us
Here was the room again where he had been
So long that something of him should be seen,
Or felt—and so it was. Incredulous,
I turned about, loath to be greeted thus,
And there he was in his old chair, serene
As ever, and as laconic and as lean
As when he lived, and as cadaverous.

Calm as he was of old when we were young,
He sat there gazing at the pallid flame
Before him. "And how far will this go on?"
I thought. He felt the failure of my tongue,
And smiled: "I was not here until you came;
And I shall not be here when you are gone."

EDWIN ARLINGTON ROBINSON

PAUL LAURENCE DUNBAR

1872–1906

Paul Laurence Dunbar's depictions of African American life during and after the Civil War have made him a controversial poet. Many readers judge his dialect poems as overly cheerful; they accuse him of encouraging stereotypes. The son of former slaves, Dunbar was the only African American student at the high school he attended in Dayton, Ohio. A popular poet in his time, Dunbar was ambivalent about his fame. He feared that his reputation was based only on his use of dialect and not on his other, more traditional work.

I did once want to be a lawyer, but that ambition has long since died out before the all-absorbing desire to be a worthy singer of the songs of God and nature. To be able to interpret my own people through song and story, and to prove to the many that after all we are more human than African.

A song is but a little thing,
And yet what joy it is to sing!
In hours of toil it gives me zest,
And when at eve I long for rest;
5   When cows come home along the bars,
      And in the fold I hear the bell,
As Night, the shepherd, herds his stars,
      I sing my song, and all is well.

There are no ears to hear my lays,
10   No lips to lift a word of praise;
But still, with faith unfaltering,
I live and laugh and love and sing.
What matters yon unheeding throng?
      They cannot feel my spirit's spell,
15   Since life is sweet and love is long,
      I sing my song, and all is well.

My days are never days of ease;
I till my ground and prune my trees.
When ripened gold is all the plain,
20   I put my sickle to the grain.
I labor hard, and toil and sweat,
      While others dream within the dell;
But even while my brow is wet,
      I sing my song, and all is well.

25   Sometimes the sun, unkindly hot,
My garden makes a desert spot;
Sometimes a blight upon the tree
Takes all my fruit away from me;
And then with throes of bitter pain
30   Rebellious passions rise and swell;
But—life is more than fruit or grain,
      And so I sing, and all is well.

The night is dewy as a maiden's mouth,
  The skies are bright as are a maiden's eyes,
  Soft as a maiden's breath the wind that flies
Up from the perfumed bosom of the South.
5 Like sentinels, the pines stand in the park;
  And hither hastening, like rakes that roam,
  With lamps to light their wayward footsteps home,
The fireflies come stagg'ring down the dark.

Dey was talkin' in de cabin, dey was talkin' in de hall;
But I listened kin' o' keerless, not a-t'inkin' 'bout it all;
An' on Sunday, too, I noticed, dey was whisp'rin' mighty much,
Stan'in' all erroun' de roadside w'en dey let us out o' chu'ch.
5   But I did n't t'ink erbout it 'twell de middle of de week,
An' my 'Lias come to see me, an' somehow he could n't speak.
Den I seed all in a minute whut he'd come to see me for;—
Dey had 'listed colo'ed sojers an' my 'Lias gwine to wah.

Oh, I hugged him, an' I kissed him, an' I baiged him not to go;
10   But he tol' me dat his conscience, hit was callin' to him so,
An' he could n't baih to lingah w'en he had a chanst to fight
For de freedom dey had gin him an' de glory of de right.
So he kissed me, an' he lef' me, w'en I 'd p'omised to be true;
An' dey put a knapsack on him, an' a coat all colo'ed blue.
15   So I gin him pap's ol' Bible f'om de bottom of de draw',—
W'en dey 'listed colo'ed sojers an' my 'Lias went to wah.

But I t'ought of all de weary miles dat he would have to tramp,
An' I could n't be contented w'en dey tuk him to de camp.
W'y my hea't nigh broke wid grievin' 'twell I seed him on de street;
20   Den I felt lak I could go an' th'ow my body at his feet.
For his buttons was a-shinin', an' his face was shinin', too,
An' he looked so strong an' mighty in his coat o' sojer blue,
Dat I hollahed, "Step up, manny," dough my th'oat was so', an' raw,—
Wen dey 'listed colo'ed sojers an' my 'Lias went to wah.

25 Ol' Mis' cried w'en mastah lef' huh, young Miss mou'ned huh brothah Ned,
I did n't know dey feelin's is de ve'y wo'ds dey said
W'en I tol' 'em I was so'y. Dey had done gin up dey all;
But dey only seemed mo' proudah dat dey men had hyeahed de call.
Bofe my mastahs went in gray suits, an' I loved de Yankee blue,
30 But I t'ought dat I could sorrer for de losin' of 'em too;
But I could n't, for I did n't know de ha'f o' whut I saw,
'Twell dey 'listed colo'ed sojers an' my 'Lias went to wah.

Mastah Jack come home all sickly; he was broke for life, dey said;
An' dey lef' my po' young mastah some'r's on de roadside,—dead.
35 W'en de women cried an' mou'ned 'em, I could feel it thoo an' thoo,
For I had a loved un fightin' in de way o' dangah, too.
Den dey tol' me dey had laid him some'r's way down souf to res',
Wid de flag dat he had fit for shinin' daih acrost his breas'.

Well, I cried, but den I reckon dat 's whut Gawd had called him for,
W'en dey 'listed colo'ed sojers an' my 'Lias went to wah.

PAUL LAURENCE DUNBAR

We wear the mask that grins and lies,
It hides our cheeks and shades our eyes,—
This debt we pay to human guile;
With torn and bleeding hearts we smile,
5   And mouth with myriad subtleties.

Why should the world be overwise,
In counting all our tears and sighs?
Nay, let them only see us, while
   We wear the mask.

10   We smile, but, O great Christ, our cries
To thee from tortured souls arise.
We sing, but oh the clay is vile
Beneath our feet, and long the mile;
But let the world dream otherwise,
   We wear the mask!

A song for the unsung heroes who rose in the country's need,
When the life of the land was threatened by the slaver's cruel greed,
For the men who came from the cornfield, who came from the plough
    and the flail,
Who rallied round when they heard the sound of the mighty man of the rail.

5   They laid them down in the valleys, they laid them down in the wood,
And the world looked on at the work they did, and whispered, "It is good."
They fought their way on the hillside, they fought their way in the glen,
And God looked down on their sinews brown, and said, "I have made
    them men."

They went to the blue lines gladly, and the blue lines took them in,
10   And the men who saw their muskets' fire thought not of their dusky skin.
The gray lines rose and melted beneath their scathing showers,
And they said, "'T is true, they have force to do, these old slave
    boys of ours."

Ah, Wagner saw their glory, and Pillow knew their blood,
That poured on a nation's altar, a sacrificial flood.
15   Port Hudson heard their war-cry that smote its smoke-filled air,
And the old free fires of their savage sires again were kindled there.

They laid them down where the rivers the greening valleys gem.
And the song of the thund'rous cannon was their sole requiem,
And the great smoke wreath that mingled its hue with the dusky cloud,
20   Was the flag that furled o'er a saddened world, and the sheet that made
    their shroud.

Oh, Mighty God of the Battles Who held them in Thy hand,
Who gave them strength through the whole day's length, to fight for their
    native land,
They are lying dead on the hillsides, they are lying dead on the plain,
And we have not fire to smite the lyre and sing them one brief strain.

25   Give, Thou, some seer the power to sing them in their might,
The men who feared the master's whip, but did not fear the fight;
That he may tell of their virtues as minstrels did of old,
Till the pride of face and the hate of race grow obsolete and cold.

A song for the unsung heroes who stood the awful test,
30   When the humblest host that the land could boast went forth to meet
    the best;
A song for the unsung heroes who fell on the bloody sod,
Who fought their way from night to day and struggled up to God.

ROBERT FROST

1874–1963

Although deeply identified as a poet—perhaps *the* poet—of New England, Robert Frost actually was born and lived his early childhood in San Francisco. As a young man, he farmed in New Hampshire but left for England in 1912 to devote himself to poetry. There he met Edward Thomas, William Butler Yeats, and other poets of the time. He published his first two books in England and then returned to the United States in 1915. In 1924, Frost won his first Pulitzer Prize in poetry, and his reputation was made. Frost's poetry combines a close attention to meter with an ear for the rhythm of everyday speech. His moment of singular public recognition was in 1961 when he read his poem "The Gift Outright" at the inauguration of President John F. Kennedy.

There is no other way to attain poetic success than by stern emotional control and absolute adherence to sincere endeavor. Slopping over isn't poetry.

MOWING

There was never a sound beside the wood but one,
And that was my long scythe whispering to the ground.
What was it it whispered? I knew not well myself;
Perhaps it was something about the heat of the sun,
5   Something, perhaps, about the lack of sound—
And that was why it whispered and did not speak.
It was no dream of the gift of idle hours,
Or easy gold at the hand of fay or elf:
Anything more than the truth would have seemed too weak
10   To the earnest love that laid the swale in rows,
Not without feeble-pointed spikes of flowers
(Pale orchises), and scared a bright green snake.
The fact is the sweetest dream that labor knows.
My long scythe whispered and left the hay to make.

"When I was just as far as I could walk
From here today,
There was an hour
All still
When leaning with my head against a flower
I heard you talk.
Don't say I didn't, for I heard you say—
You spoke from that flower on the windowsill—
Do you remember what it was you said?"

"First tell me what it was you thought you heard."

"Having found the flower and driven a bee away,
I leaned my head,
And holding by the stalk,
I listened and I thought I caught the word—
What was it? Did you call me by my name?
Or did you say—
Someone said 'Come'—I heard it as I bowed."

"I may have thought as much, but not aloud."

"Well, so I came."

1. LONELINESS

Her Word

One ought not to have to care
    So much as you and I
Care when the birds come round the house
    To seem to say good-by;

5   Or care so much when they come back
    With whatever it is they sing;
The truth being we are as much
    Too glad for the one thing

As we are too sad for the other here—
10   With birds that fill their breasts
But with each other and themselves
    And their built or driven nests.

2. HOUSE FEAR

Always—I tell you this they learned—
Always at night when they returned
15   To the lonely house from far away,
To lamps unlighted and fire gone gray,
They learned to rattle the lock and key
To give whatever might chance to be,
Warning and time to be off in flight:
20   And preferring the out- to the indoor night,
They learned to leave the house door wide
Until they had lit the lamp inside.

3. THE SMILE

Her Word

I didn't like the way he went away.
That smile! It never came of being gay.
25 Still he smiled—did you see him?—I was sure!
Perhaps because we gave him only bread
And the wretch knew from that that we were poor.
Perhaps because he let us give instead
Of seizing from us as he might have seized.
30 Perhaps he mocked at us for being wed,
Or being very young (and he was pleased
To have a vision of us old and dead).
I wonder how far down the road he's got.
He's watching from the woods as like as not.

4. THE OFT-REPEATED DREAM

35 She had no saying dark enough
    For the dark pine that kept
Forever trying the window latch
    Of the room where they slept.

The tireless but ineffectual hands
40   That with every futile pass
Made the great tree seem as a little bird
    Before the mystery of glass!

It never had been inside the room,
    And only one of the two
45 Was afraid in an oft-repeated dream
    Of what the tree might do.

5. THE IMPULSE

It was too lonely for her there,
    And too wild,
And since there were but two of them,
50   And no child,

And work was little in the house,
    She was free,
And followed where he furrowed field,
    Or felled tree.

55 She rested on a log and tossed
    The fresh chips,
With a song only to herself
    On her lips.

And once she went to break a bough
60   Of black alder.
She strayed so far she scarcely heard
    When he called her—

And didn't answer—didn't speak—
    Or return.
65 She stood, and then she ran and hid
    In the fern.

He never found her, though he looked
    Everywhere,
And he asked at her mother's house
70   Was she there.

Sudden and swift and light as that
    The ties gave,
And he learned of finalities
    Besides the grave.

The buzz saw snarled and rattled in the yard
And made dust and dropped stove-length sticks of wood,
Sweet-scented stuff when the breeze drew across it.
And from there those that lifted eyes could count

5   Five mountain ranges one behind the other
Under the sunset far into Vermont.
And the saw snarled and rattled, snarled and rattled,
As it ran light, or had to bear a load.
And nothing happened: day was all but done.

10   Call it a day, I wish they might have said
To please the boy by giving him the half hour
That a boy counts so much when saved from work.
His sister stood beside them in her apron
To tell them "Supper." At the word, the saw,

15   As if to prove saws knew what supper meant,
Leaped out at the boy's hand, or seemed to leap—
He must have given the hand. However it was,
Neither refused the meeting. But the hand!
The boy's first outcry was a rueful laugh,

20   As he swung toward them holding up the hand,
Half in appeal, but half as if to keep
The life from spilling. Then the boy saw all—
Since he was old enough to know, big boy
Doing a man's work, though a child at heart—

25   He saw all spoiled. "Don't let him cut my hand off—
The doctor, when he comes. Don't let him, sister!"
So. But the hand was gone already.
The doctor put him in the dark of ether.
He lay and puffed his lips out with his breath.

30   And then—the watcher at his pulse took fright.
No one believed. They listened at his heart.
Little—less—nothing!—and that ended it.
No more to build on there. And they, since they
Were not the one dead, turned to their affairs.

I have been one acquainted with the night.
I have walked out in rain—and back in rain.
I have outwalked the furthest city light.

I have looked down the saddest city lane.
I have passed by the watchman on his beat
And dropped my eyes, unwilling to explain.

I have stood still and stopped the sound of feet
When far away an interrupted cry
Came over houses from another street,

But not to call me back or say good-by;
And further still at an unearthly height
One luminary clock against the sky

Proclaimed the time was neither wrong nor right.
I have been one acquainted with the night.

DESERT PLACES

Snow falling and night falling fast, oh, fast
In a field I looked into going past,
And the ground almost covered smooth in snow,
But a few weeds and stubble showing last.

5   The woods around it have it—it is theirs.
All animals are smothered in their lairs.
I am too absent-spirited to count;
The loneliness includes me unawares.

And lonely as it is, that loneliness
10 Will be more lonely ere it will be less—
A blanker whiteness of benighted snow
With no expression, nothing to express.

They cannot scare me with their empty spaces
Between stars—on stars where no human race is.
15 I have it in me so much nearer home
To scare myself with my own desert places.

She drew back; he was calm:
"It is this that had the power."
And he lashed his open palm
With the tender-headed flower.
5   He smiled for her to smile,
But she was either blind
Or willfully unkind.
He eyed her for a while
For a woman and a puzzle.
10   He flicked and flung the flower,
And another sort of smile
Caught up like fingertips
The corners of his lips
And cracked his ragged muzzle.
15   She was standing to the waist
In goldenrod and brake,
Her shining hair displaced.
He stretched her either arm
As if she made it ache
20   To clasp her—not to harm;
As if he could not spare
To touch her neck and hair.
"If this has come to us
And not to me alone——"
25   So she thought she heard him say;
Though with every word he spoke
His lips were sucked and blown
And the effort made him choke
Like a tiger at a bone.
30   She had to lean away.
She dared not stir a foot,
Lest movement should provoke

The demon of pursuit
That slumbers in a brute.
35 It was then her mother's call
From inside the garden wall
Made her steal a look of fear
To see if he could hear
And would pounce to end it all
40 Before her mother came.
She looked and saw the shame:
A hand hung like a paw,
An arm worked like a saw
As if to be persuasive,
45 An ingratiating laugh
That cut the snout in half,
An eye become evasive.
A girl could only see
That a flower had marred a man,
50 But what she could not see
Was that the flower might be
Other than base and fetid:
That the flower had done but part,
And what the flower began
55 Her own too meager heart
Had terribly completed.
She looked and saw the worst.
And the dog or what it was,
Obeying bestial laws,
60 A coward save at night,
Turned from the place and ran.
She heard him stumble first
And use his hands in flight.
She heard him bark outright.

65   And oh, for one so young
        The bitter words she spit
        Like some tenacious bit
        That will not leave the tongue.
        She plucked her lips for it,
70   And still the horror clung.
        Her mother wiped the foam
        From her chin, picked up her comb,
        And drew her backward home.

It is getting dark and time he drew to a house,
But the blizzard blinds him to any house ahead.
The storm gets down his neck in an icy souse
That sucks his breath like a wicked cat in bed.

5   The snow blows on him and off him, exerting force
Downward to make him sit astride a drift,
Imprint a saddle, and calmly consider a course.
He peers out shrewdly into the thick and swift.

Since he means to come to a door he will come to a door,
10   Although so compromised of aim and rate
He may fumble wide of the knob a yard or more,
And to those concerned he may seem a little late.

WALLACE STEVENS

1879–1955

Wallace Stevens's "day job" as vice president of the Hartford Accident and Indemnity Company makes an interesting contrast to his whimsical, often cerebral, slightly surreal poetry. Stevens himself saw no contradiction, remarking that surety claims and poetry have much in common and that holding another job gives a poet character. He published his first poems in 1914, at the age of thirty-five, and his first volume of poetry in 1923. A modest man, Stevens rarely mentioned his literary reputation to colleagues or business associates. He spoke of poetry as "a supreme fiction," an act or creation of the imagination that proposes the possibility of fulfillment and provides "a freshening of life," ultimately a replacement for religion, a secular scripture for a godless age.

There's nothing to that saying that poets are born.
They're not born in particular. Everyone is born.
Some of those who are born are interested
in poetry, that's all.

I have finished my combat with the sun;
And my body, the old animal,
Knows nothing more.

The powerful seasons bred and killed,
5   And were themselves the genii
Of their own ends.

Oh, but the very self of the storm
Of sun and slaves, breeding and death,
The old animal,

10   The senses and feeling, the very sound
And sight, and all there was of the storm,
Knows nothing more.

I placed a jar in Tennessee,
And round it was, upon a hill.
It made the slovenly wilderness
Surround that hill.

5   The wilderness rose up to it,
And sprawled around, no longer wild.
The jar was round upon the ground
And tall and of a port in air.

It took dominion everywhere.
10   The jar was gray and bare.
It did not give of bird or bush,
Like nothing else in Tennessee.

FROGS EAT BUTTERFLIES. SNAKES EAT FROGS.
HOGS EAT SNAKES. MEN EAT HOGS

It is true that the rivers went nosing like swine,
Tugging at banks, until they seemed
Bland belly-sounds in somnolent troughs,

That the air was heavy with the breath of these swine,
5   The breath of turgid summer, and
Heavy with thunder's rattapallax,

That the man who erected this cabin, planted
This field, and tended it awhile,
Knew not the quirks of imagery,

10   That the hours of his indolent, arid days,
Grotesque with this nosing in banks,
This somnolence and rattapallax,

Seemed to suckle themselves on his arid being,
As the swine-like rivers suckled themselves
While they went seaward to the sea-mouths.

1

Among twenty snowy mountains,
The only moving thing
Was the eye of the blackbird.

2

I was of three minds,
Like a tree
In which there are three blackbirds.

3

The blackbird whirled in the autumn winds.
It was a small part of the pantomime.

4

A man and a woman
Are one.
A man and a woman and a blackbird
Are one.

5

I do not know which to prefer,
The beauty of inflections
Or the beauty of innuendoes,
The blackbird whistling
Or just after.

6

Icicles filled the long window
With barbaric glass.
20   The shadow of the blackbird
Crossed it, to and fro.
The mood
Traced in the shadow
An indecipherable cause.

7

25   O thin men of Haddam,
Why do you imagine golden birds?
Do you not see how the blackbird
Walks around the feet
Of the women about you?

8

30   I know noble accents
And lucid, inescapable rhythms;
But I know, too,
That the blackbird is involved
In what I know.

9

35   When the blackbird flew out of sight,
It marked the edge
Of one of many circles.

10

At the sight of blackbirds
Flying in a green light,
Even the bawds of euphony
Would cry out sharply.

11

He rode over Connecticut
In a glass coach.
Once, a fear pierced him,
In that he mistook
The shadow of his equipage
For blackbirds.

12

The river is moving.
The blackbird must be flying.

13

It was evening all afternoon.
It was snowing
And it was going to snow.
The blackbird sat
In the cedar-limbs.

40

45

50

Last evening the moon rose above this rock
Impure upon a world unpurged.
The man and his companion stopped
To rest before the heroic height.

5 Coldly the wind fell upon them
In many majesties of sound:
They that had left the flame-freaked sun
To seek a sun of fuller fire.

Instead there was this tufted rock
10 Massively rising high and bare
Beyond all trees, the ridges thrown
Like giant arms among the clouds.

There was neither voice nor crested image,
No chorister, nor priest. There was
15 Only the great height of the rock
And the two of them standing still to rest.

There was the cold wind and the sound
It made, away from the muck of the land
That they had left, heroic sound
Joyous and jubilant and sure.

1

Clear water in a brilliant bowl,
Pink and white carnations. The light
In the room more like a snowy air,
Reflecting snow. A newly-fallen snow
5   At the end of winter when afternoons return.
Pink and white carnations—one desires
So much more than that. The day itself
Is simplified: a bowl of white,
Cold, a cold porcelain, low and round,
10   With nothing more than the carnations there.

2

Say even that this complete simplicity
Stripped one of all one's torments, concealed
The evilly compounded, vital I
And made it fresh in a world of white,
15   A world of clear water, brilliant-edged,
Still one would want more, one would need more,
More than a world of white and snowy scents.

3

There would still remain the never-resting mind,
So that one would want to escape, come back
20   To what had been so long composed.
The imperfect is our paradise.
Note that, in this bitterness, delight,
Since the imperfect is so hot in us,
Lies in flawed words and stubborn sounds.

1

Opusculum paedagogum.
The pears are not viols,
Nudes or bottles.
They resemble nothing else.

2

5   They are yellow forms
Composed of curves
Bulging toward the base.
They are touched red.

3

They are not flat surfaces
10   Having curved outlines.
They are round
Tapering toward the top.

4

In the way they are modelled
There are bits of blue.
15   A hard dry leaf hangs
From the stem.

5

The yellow glistens.
It glistens with various yellows,
Citrons, oranges and greens
20   Flowering over the skin.

6

The shadows of the pears
Are blobs on the green cloth.
The pears are not seen
As the observer wills.

She sang beyond the genius of the sea.
The water never formed to mind or voice,
Like a body wholly body, fluttering
Its empty sleeves; and yet its mimic motion
5   Made constant cry, caused constantly a cry,
That was not ours although we understood,
Inhuman, of the veritable ocean.

The sea was not a mask. No more was she.
The song and water were not medleyed sound
10   Even if what she sang was what she heard,
Since what she sang was uttered word by word.
It may be that in all her phrases stirred
The grinding water and the gasping wind;
But it was she and not the sea we heard.

15   For she was the maker of the song she sang.
The ever-hooded, tragic-gestured sea
Was merely a place by which she walked to sing.
Whose spirit is this? we said, because we knew
It was the spirit that we sought and knew
20   That we should ask this often as she sang.

If it was only the dark voice of the sea
That rose, or even colored by many waves;
If it was only the outer voice of sky
And cloud, of the sunken coral water-walled,
25   However clear, it would have been deep air,
The heaving speech of air, a summer sound
Repeated in a summer without end
And sound alone. But it was more than that,
More even than her voice, and ours, among
30   The meaningless plungings of water and the wind,
Theatrical distances, bronze shadows heaped
On high horizons, mountainous atmospheres
Of sky and sea.

                    It was her voice that made
35   The sky acutest at its vanishing.
She measured to the hour its solitude.
She was the single artificer of the world
In which she sang. And when she sang, the sea,
Whatever self it had, became the self
40   That was her song, for she was the maker. Then we,
As we beheld her striding there alone,
Knew that there never was a world for her
Except the one she sang and, singing, made.

WALLACE STEVENS

Ramon Fernandez, tell me, if you know,
Why, when the singing ended and we turned
Toward the town, tell why the glassy lights,
The lights in the fishing boats at anchor there,
As the night descended, tilting in the air,
Mastered the night and portioned out the sea,
Fixing emblazoned zones and fiery poles,
Arranging, deepening, enchanting night.

Oh! Blessed rage for order, pale Ramon,
The maker's rage to order words of the sea,
Words of the fragrant portals, dimly-starred,
And of ourselves and of our origins,
In ghostlier demarcations, keener sounds.

The palm at the end of the mind,
Beyond the last thought, rises
In the bronze decor,

A gold-feathered bird
5   Sings in the palm, without human meaning,
Without human feeling, a foreign song.

You know then that it is not the reason
That makes us happy or unhappy.
The bird sings. Its feathers shine.

10   The palm stands on the edge of space.
The wind moves slowly in the branches.
The bird's fire-fangled feathers dangle down.

WILLIAM CARLOS WILLIAMS

1883–1963

William Carlos Williams was born in Rutherford, New Jersey, to an English father and a Puerto Rican mother; the primary language of the household was Spanish. Williams lived his entire life—writing, practicing medicine (delivering nearly three thousand babies), and raising a family—in Rutherford. Williams worked to capture American idioms in his poetry. He felt that poems should emerge from a profound sense of place—the local. His early poems are spare and lean, while the later poems demonstrate a wide range of variation and complexity. In the 1950s, the beat poets identified Williams as one of their progenitors, and he wrote the introduction to Allen Ginsberg's *Howl and Other Poems*. The literary establishment, however, was slow in recognizing Williams's achievement as a writer; he was posthumously awarded the Pulitzer Prize for *Pictures from Brueghel*.

> How can we accept Einstein's theory of relativity, affecting
> our very conception of the heavens about us of which
> poets write so much, without incorporating its essential
> fact—the relativity of measurements—into our own
> category of activity: the poem.

TO WAKEN AN OLD LADY

Old age is
a flight of small
cheeping birds
skimming
5   bare trees
above a snow glaze.
Gaining and failing
they are buffeted
by a dark wind—
10   But what?
On harsh weedstalks
the flock has rested,
the snow
is covered with broken
15   seedhusks
and the wind tempered
by a shrill
piping of plenty.

At ten A.M. the young housewife
moves about in negligee behind
the wooden walls of her husband's house.
I pass solitary in my car.

5   Then again she comes to the curb
to call the ice-man, fish-man, and stands
shy, uncorseted, tucking in
stray ends of hair, and I compare her
to a fallen leaf.

10   The noiseless wheels of my car
rush with a crackling sound over
dried leaves as I bow and pass smiling.

Her body is not so white as
anemone petals nor so smooth—nor
so remote a thing. It is a field
of the wild carrot taking
5 the field by force; the grass
does not raise above it.
Here is no question of whiteness,
white as can be, with a purple mole
at the center of each flower.
10 Each flower is a hand's span
of her whiteness. Wherever
his hand has lain there is
a tiny purple blemish. Each part
is a blossom under his touch
15 to which the fibres of her being
stem one by one, each to its end,
until the whole field is a
white desire, empty, a single stem,
a cluster, flower by flower,
20 a pious wish to whiteness gone over—
or nothing.

Sorrow is my own yard
where the new grass
flames as it has flamed
often before but not
5 with the cold fire
that closes round me this year.
Thirtyfive years
I lived with my husband.
The plumtree is white today
10 with masses of flowers.
Masses of flowers
load the cherry branches
and color some bushes
yellow and some red
15 but the grief in my heart
is stronger than they
for though they were my joy
formerly, today I notice them
and turned away forgetting.
20 Today my son told me
that in the meadows,
at the edge of the heavy woods
in the distance, he saw
trees of white flowers.
25 I feel that I would like
to go there
and fall into those flowers
and sink into the marsh near them.

By the road to the contagious hospital
under the surge of the blue
mottled clouds driven from the
northeast—a cold wind. Beyond, the
5   waste of broad, muddy fields
brown with dried weeds, standing and fallen

patches of standing water
the scattering of tall trees

All along the road the reddish
10   purplish, forked, upstanding, twiggy
stuff of bushes and small trees
with dead, brown leaves under them
leafless vines—

Lifeless in appearance, sluggish
15   dazed spring approaches—

They enter the new world naked,
cold, uncertain of all
save that they enter. All about them
the cold, familiar wind—

20   Now the grass, tomorrow
the stiff curl of wildcarrot leaf

One by one objects are defined—
It quickens: clarity, outline of leaf

But now the stark dignity of
25   entrance—Still, the profound change
has come upon them: rooted, they
grip down and begin to awaken

THE GREAT FIGURE

Among the rain
and lights
I saw the figure 5
in gold
5   on a red
firetruck
moving
tense
unheeded
10   to gong clangs
siren howls
and wheels rumbling
through the dark city.

I have eaten
the plums
that were in
the icebox

5   and which
you were probably
saving
for breakfast

Forgive me
10   they were delicious
so sweet
and so cold

THE LAST WORDS OF MY ENGLISH GRANDMOTHER

There were some dirty plates
and a glass of milk
beside her on a small table
near the rank, disheveled bed—

5   Wrinkled and nearly blind
she lay and snored
rousing with anger in her tones
to cry for food,

Gimme something to eat—
10   They're starving me—
I'm all right I won't go
to the hospital. No, no, no

Give me something to eat
Let me take you
15   to the hospital, I said
and after you are well

you can do as you please.
She smiled, Yes
you do what you please first
20   then I can do what I please—

Oh, oh, oh! she cried
as the ambulance men lifted
her to the stretcher—
Is this what you call

25   making me comfortable?
By now her mind was clear—
Oh you think you're smart
you young people,

she said, but I'll tell you
30   you don't know anything.
Then we started.
On the way

we passed a long row
of elms. She looked at them
35   awhile out of
the ambulance window and said,

What are all those
fuzzy-looking things out there?
Trees? Well, I'm tired
of them and rolled her head away.

LANDSCAPE WITH THE FALL OF ICARUS

According to Brueghel
when Icarus fell
it was spring

a farmer was ploughing
his field
the whole pageantry

of the year was
awake tingling
near

the edge of the sea
concerned
with itself

sweating in the sun
that melted
the wings' wax

unsignificantly
off the coast
there was

a splash quite unnoticed
this was
Icarus drowning

so much depends
upon

a red wheel
barrow

5 glazed with rain
water

beside the white
chickens

WILLIAM CARLOS WILLIAMS

The descent beckons
        as the ascent beckoned.
                Memory is a kind
of accomplishment,
        a sort of renewal
                even
an initiation, since the spaces it opens are new places
        inhabited by hordes
                heretofore unrealized,
of new kinds—
        since their movements
                are toward new objectives
(even though formerly they were abandoned).

No defeat is made up entirely of defeat—since
the world it opens is always a place
        formerly
                unsuspected. A
world lost,
        a world unsuspected,
                beckons to new places
and no whiteness (lost) is so white as the memory
of whiteness

With evening, love wakens
        though its shadows
                which are alive by reason
of the sun shining—
        grow sleepy now and drop away
                from desire

Love without shadows stirs now
            beginning to awaken
                        as night
advances.

The descent
            made up of despairs
                      and without accomplishment
realizes a new awakening:
                  which is a reversal
of despair.
            For what we cannot accomplish, what
is denied to love,
            what we have lost in the anticipation—
                a descent follows,
endless and indestructible

H. D.

1886–1961

Born Hilda Doolittle, H. D. was given her pen name by her friend and occasional fiancé, Ezra Pound. She traveled to Europe in 1911 and stayed abroad the rest of her life. Along with Pound, H. D. helped to advance the imagist movement in poetry, a style characterized by precise, concrete images and experimental rhythms. Her romantic and personal life was often traumatic. She experienced several breakdowns and became Sigmund Freud's patient in 1933. Although she maintained friendships with most of the prominent literary figures of her day, H. D. herself was not widely known during her lifetime.

I consider this business of writing a very sacred thing!

O be swift—
we have always known you wanted us.

We fled inland with our flocks,
we pastured them in hollows,
5   cut off from the wind
and the salt track of the marsh.

We worshipped inland—
we stepped past wood-flowers,
we forgot your tang,
10   we brushed wood-grass.

We wandered from pine-hills
through oak and scrub-oak tangles,
we broke hyssop and bramble,
we caught flower and new bramble-fruit
15   in our hair: we laughed
as each branch whipped back,
we tore our feet in half-buried rocks
and knotted roots and acorn-cups.

We forgot—we worshipped,
20   we parted green from green,
we sought further thickets,
we dipped our ankles
through leaf-mold and earth,
and wood and wood-bank enchanted us—
25   and the feel of the clefts in the bark,
and the slope between tree and tree—
and a slender path strung field to field
and wood to wood
and hill to hill
30   and the forest after it.

We forgot for a moment;
tree-resin, tree-bark,
sweat of a torn branch
were sweet to the taste.

35 We were enchanted with the fields,
the tufts of coarse grass—
in the shorter grass—
we loved all this.

But now, our boat climbs—hesitates—
       drops—
40 climbs—hesitates—crawls back—
climbs—hesitates—
O, be swift—
we have always known you wanted us.

Chance says,
come here,
chance says,
can you bear

5   to part?
chance says,
sweetheart,
we haven't loved

for almost a year,
10   can you bear
this loneliness?
I can't;

apart from you,
I fear
15   wind,
bird,

sea,
wave,
low places
20   and the high air;

I hear
dire threat
everywhere;
I start

25   at wind
in sycamores,
I can't bear
anything

further;

30 chance says,
dear,
I'm here,

don't you want me
any more?

FRAGMENT 113

Neither honey nor bee for me. —Sappho

Not honey,
not the plunder of the bee
from meadow or sand-flower
or mountain bush;
5   from winter-flower or shoot
born of the later heat:
not honey, not the sweet
stain on the lips and teeth:
not honey, not the deep
10   plunge of soft belly
and the clinging of the gold-edged
pollen-dusted feet;

not so—
though rapture blind my eyes,
15   and hunger crisp
dark and inert my mouth,
not honey, not the south,
not the tall stalk
of red twin-lilies,
20   nor light branch of fruit tree
caught in flexible light branch;

not honey, not the south;
ah flower of purple iris,
flower of white,
25   or of the iris, withering the grass—
for fleck of the sun's fire,
gathers such heat and power,
that shadow-print is light,
cast through the petals
30   of the yellow iris flower;

not iris—old desire—old passion—
old forgetfulness—old pain—
not this, nor any flower,
but if you turn again,
35   seek strength of arm and throat,
touch as the god;
neglect the lyre-note;
knowing that you shall feel,
about the frame,
40   no trembling of the string
but heat, more passionate
of bone and the white shell
and fiery tempered steel.

H. D.

Nor skin nor hide nor fleece
    shall cover you,
nor curtain of crimson nor fine
shelter of cedar-wood be over you,
5   nor the fir-tree
      nor the pine.

Nor sight of whin nor gorse
    nor river-yew,
nor fragrance of flowering bush,
10   nor wailing of reed-bird to waken you,
      nor of linnet,
      nor of thrush.

Nor word nor touch nor sight
    of lover, you
15   shall long through the night but for this:
the roll of the full tide to cover you
      without question,
      without kiss.

Where the slow river
meets the tide,
a red swan lifts red wings
and darker beak,
5   and underneath the purple down
of his soft breast
uncurls his coral feet.

Through the deep purple
of the dying heat
10   of sun and mist,
the level ray of sun-beam
has caressed
the lily with dark breast,
and flecked with richer gold
15   its golden crest.

Where the slow lifting
of the tide,
floats into the river
and slowly drifts
20   among the reeds,
and lifts the yellow flags,
he floats
where tide and river meet.

H. D.

Ah kingly kiss—
25 no more regret
nor old deep memories
to mar the bliss;
where the low sedge is thick,
the gold day-lily
30 outspreads and rests
beneath soft fluttering
of red swan wings
and the warm quivering
of the red swan's breast.

T. S. ELIOT

1888–1965

The seventh child in a wealthy family, T. S. Eliot became an immensely influential figure in modern poetry, as well as a successful playwright, literary critic, and editor. Educated at Harvard, he spent a year in Paris and moved to England in 1914, eventually becoming a British citizen. His first book of poetry was published in 1917 and immediately established him as a leader of the avant-garde. Many people consider "The Waste Land," published in 1922, to be the most influential work in twentieth-century poetry. Eliot was awarded the Nobel Prize in literature in 1948.

Poetry is not a turning loose of emotion, but an escape from emotion; it is not the expression of personality, but an escape from personality.

S'io credessi che mia risposta fosse
a persona che mai tornasse al mondo,
questa fiamma staria senza più scosse.
Ma per ciò che giammai di questo fondo
non tornò vivo alcun, s'i'odo il vero,
senza tema d'infamia ti rispondo.

Let us go then, you and I,
When the evening is spread out against the sky
Like a patient etherised upon a table;
Let us go, through certain half-deserted streets,
5   The muttering retreats
Of restless nights in one-night cheap hotels
And sawdust restaurants with oyster-shells:
Streets that follow like a tedious argument
Of insidious intent
10   To lead you to an overwhelming question．．．
Oh, do not ask, "What is it?"
Let us go and make our visit.

In the room the women come and go
Talking of Michelangelo.

15   The yellow fog that rubs its back upon the window-panes,
The yellow smoke that rubs its muzzle on the window-panes,
Licked its tongue into the corners of the evening,
Lingered upon the pools that stand in drains,
Let fall upon its back the soot that falls from chimneys,
20   Slipped by the terrace, made a sudden leap,
And seeing that it was a soft October night,
Curled once about the house, and fell asleep.

And indeed there will be time
For the yellow smoke that slides along the street
Rubbing its back upon the window-panes;
There will be time, there will be time
To prepare a face to meet the faces that you meet;
There will be time to murder and create,
And time for all the works and days of hands
That lift and drop a question on your plate;
Time for you and time for me,
And time yet for a hundred indecisions,
And for a hundred visions and revisions,
Before the taking of a toast and tea.

In the room the women come and go
Talking of Michelangelo.

And indeed there will be time
To wonder, "Do I dare?" and, "Do I dare?"
Time to turn back and descend the stair,
With a bald spot in the middle of my hair—
(They will say: "How his hair is growing thin!")
My morning coat, my collar mounting firmly to the chin,
My necktie rich and modest, but asserted by a simple pin—
(They will say: "But how his arms and legs are thin!")
Do I dare
Disturb the universe?
In a minute there is time
For decisions and revisions which a minute will reverse.

T. S. ELIOT

For I have known them all already, known them all—

50 Have known the evenings, mornings, afternoons,
I have measured out my life with coffee spoons;
I know the voices dying with a dying fall
Beneath the music from a farther room.
     So how should I presume?

55 And I have known the eyes already, known them all—
The eyes that fix you in a formulated phrase,
And when I am formulated, sprawling on a pin,
When I am pinned and wriggling on the wall,
Then how should I begin
60 To spit out all the butt-ends of my days and ways?
     And how should I presume?

And I have known the arms already, known them all—
Arms that are braceleted and white and bare
(But in the lamplight, downed with light brown hair!)
65 Is it perfume from a dress
That makes me so digress?
Arms that lie along a table, or wrap about a shawl.
     And should I then presume?
     And how should I begin?

70 Shall I say, I have gone at dusk through narrow streets
And watched the smoke that rises from the pipes
Of lonely men in shirt-sleeves, leaning out of windows? . . .

I should have been a pair of ragged claws
Scuttling across the floors of silent seas.

75 And the afternoon, the evening, sleeps so peacefully!
Smoothed by long fingers,
Asleep . . . tired . . . or it malingers,
Stretched on the floor, here beside you and me.
Should I, after tea and cakes and ices,
80 Have the strength to force the moment to its crisis?
But though I have wept and fasted, wept and prayed,
Though I have seen my head (grown slightly bald) brought in
      upon a platter,
I am no prophet—and here's no great matter;
I have seen the moment of my greatness flicker,
85 And I have seen the eternal Footman hold my coat, and snicker,
And in short, I was afraid.

And would it have been worth it, after all,
After the cups, the marmalade, the tea,
Among the porcelain, among some talk of you and me,
Would it have been worth while,
To have bitten off the matter with a smile,
To have squeezed the universe into a ball
To roll it towards some overwhelming question,
To say: "I am Lazarus, come from the dead,
Come back to tell you all, I shall tell you all"—
If one, settling a pillow by her head,
    Should say: "That is not what I meant at all.
    That is not it, at all."

And would it have been worth it, after all,
Would it have been worth while,
After the sunsets and the dooryards and the sprinkled streets,
After the novels, after the teacups, after the skirts that trail along
    the floor—
And this, and so much more?—
It is impossible to say just what I mean!
But as if a magic lantern threw the nerves in patterns on a screen:
Would it have been worth while
If one, settling a pillow or throwing off a shawl,
And turning toward the window, should say:
    "That is not it at all,
    That is not what I meant, at all."

No! I am not Prince Hamlet, nor was meant to be;
Am an attendant lord, one that will do
To swell a progress, start a scene or two,
Advise the prince; no doubt, an easy tool,
115 Deferential, glad to be of use,
Politic, cautious, and meticulous;
Full of high sentence, but a bit obtuse;
At times, indeed, almost ridiculous—
Almost, at times, the Fool.

120 I grow old . . . I grow old . . .
I shall wear the bottoms of my trousers rolled.

Shall I part my hair behind? Do I dare to eat a peach?
I shall wear white flannel trousers, and walk upon the beach.
I have heard the mermaids singing, each to each.

125 I do not think that they will sing to me.

I have seen them riding seaward on the waves
Combing the white hair of the waves blown back
When the wind blows the water white and black.

We have lingered in the chambers of the sea
130 By sea-girls wreathed with seaweed red and brown
Till human voices wake us, and we drown.

1

The winter evening settles down
With smell of steaks in passageways.
Six o'clock.
The burnt-out ends of smoky days.
5   And now a gusty shower wraps
The grimy scraps
Of withered leaves about your feet
And newspapers from vacant lots;
The showers beat
10   On broken blinds and chimney-pots,
And at the corner of the street
A lonely cab-horse steams and stamps.

And then the lighting of the lamps.

2

The morning comes to consciousness
15   Of faint stale smells of beer
From the sawdust-trampled street
With all its muddy feet that press
To early coffee-stands.

With the other masquerades
20   That time resumes,
One thinks of all the hands
That are raising dingy shades
In a thousand furnished rooms.

3

You tossed a blanket from the bed,
You lay upon your back, and waited;
You dozed, and watched the night revealing
The thousand sordid images
Of which your soul was constituted;
They flickered against the ceiling.
And when all the world came back
And the light crept up between the shutters
And you heard the sparrows in the gutters,
You had such a vision of the street
As the street hardly understands;
Sitting along the bed's edge, where
You curled the papers from your hair,
Or clasped the yellow soles of feet
In the palms of both soiled hands.

4

His soul stretched tight across the skies
That fade behind a city block,
Or trampled by insistent feet
At four and five and six o'clock;
And short square fingers stuffing pipes,
And evening newspapers, and eyes
Assured of certain certainties,
The conscience of a blackened street
Impatient to assume the world.

T. S. ELIOT

I am moved by fancies that are curled
Around these images, and cling:
50 The notion of some infinitely gentle
Infinitely suffering thing.

Wipe your hand across your mouth, and laugh;
The worlds revolve like ancient women
Gathering fuel in vacant lots.

Twelve o'clock.
Along the reaches of the street
Held in a lunar synthesis,
Whispering lunar incantations
Dissolve the floors of memory
And all its clear relations,
Its divisions and precisions.
Every street lamp that I pass
Beats like a fatalistic drum,
And through the spaces of the dark
Midnight shakes the memory
As a madman shakes a dead geranium.

Half-past one,
The street-lamp sputtered,
The street-lamp muttered,
The street-lamp said, "Regard that woman
Who hesitates toward you in the light of the door
Which opens on her like a grin.
You see the border of her dress
Is torn and stained with sand,
And you see the corner of her eye
Twists like a crooked pin."

The memory throws up high and dry
A crowd of twisted things;
A twisted branch upon the beach
Eaten smooth, and polished
As if the world gave up
The secret of its skeleton,
Stiff and white.
A broken spring in a factory yard,
Rust that clings to the form that the strength has left
Hard and curled and ready to snap.

Half-past two,
The street-lamp said,
"Remark the cat which flattens itself in the gutter,
Slips out its tongue
And devours a morsel of rancid butter."
So the hand of the child, automatic,
Slipped out and pocketed a toy that was running along the quay.
I could see nothing behind that child's eye.
I have seen eyes in the street
Trying to peer through lighted shutters,
And a crab one afternoon in a pool,
An old crab with barnacles on his back,
Gripped the end of a stick which I held him.

Half-past three,
The lamp sputtered,
The lamp muttered in the dark.
The lamp hummed:
50 "Regard the moon,
La lune ne garde aucune rancune,
She winks a feeble eye,
She smiles into corners.
She smooths the hair of the grass.
55 The moon has lost her memory.
A washed-out smallpox cracks her face,
Her hand twists a paper rose,
That smells of dust and eau de Cologne,
She is alone
60 With all the old nocturnal smells
That cross and cross across her brain."
The reminiscence comes
Of sunless dry geraniums
And dust in crevices,
65 Smells of chestnuts in the streets,
And female smells in shuttered rooms,
And cigarettes in corridors
And cocktail smells in bars.

The lamp said,
70 "Four o'clock,
Here is the number on the door.
Memory!
You have the key,
The little lamp spreads a ring on the stair.
75 Mount.
The bed is open; the tooth-brush hangs on the wall,
Put your shoes at the door, sleep, prepare for life."

The last twist of the knife.

Miss Helen Slingsby was my maiden aunt,
And lived in a small house near a fashionable square
Cared for by servants to the number of four.
Now when she died there was silence in heaven
5   And silence at her end of the street.
The shutters were drawn and the undertaker wiped his feet—
He was aware that this sort of thing had occurred before.
The dogs were handsomely provided for,
But shortly afterwards the parrot died too.
10   The Dresden clock continued ticking on the mantelpiece,
And the footman sat upon the dining-table
Holding the second housemaid on his knees—
Who had always been so careful while her mistress lived.

A penny for the Old Guy

1

We are the hollow men
We are the stuffed men
Leaning together
Headpiece filled with straw. Alas!
5   Our dried voices, when
We whisper together
Are quiet and meaningless
As wind in dry grass
Or rats' feet over broken glass
10   In our dry cellar

Shape without form, shade without colour,
Paralysed force, gesture without motion;

Those who have crossed
With direct eyes, to death's other Kingdom
15   Remember us—if at all—not as lost
Violent souls, but only
As the hollow men
The stuffed men.

2

Eyes I dare not meet in dreams
20 In death's dream kingdom
These do not appear:
There, the eyes are
Sunlight on a broken column
There, is a tree swinging
25 And voices are
In the wind's singing
More distant and more solemn
Than a fading star.

Let me be no nearer
30 In death's dream kingdom
Let me also wear
Such deliberate disguises
Rat's coat, crowskin, crossed staves
In a field
35 Behaving as the wind behaves
No nearer—

Not that final meeting
In the twilight kingdom

3

This is the dead land
40   This is cactus land
Here the stone images
Are raised, here they receive
The supplication of a dead man's hand
Under the twinkle of a fading star.

45   Is it like this
In death's other kingdom
Waking alone
At the hour when we are
Trembling with tenderness
50   Lips that would kiss
Form prayers to broken stone

4

The eyes are not here
There are no eyes here
In this valley of dying stars
55   In this hollow valley
This broken jaw of our lost kingdoms

In this last of meeting places
We grope together
And avoid speech
60   Gathered on this beach of the tumid river

Sightless, unless
The eyes reappear
As the perpetual star
Multifoliate rose
65 Of death's twilight kingdom
The hope only
Of empty men.

5

Here we go round the prickly pear
Prickly pear prickly pear
70 *Here we go round the prickly pear*
At five o'clock in the morning.

Between the idea
And the reality
Between the motion
75 And the act
Falls the Shadow
                    For Thine is the Kingdom

Between the inception
And the creation
80 Between the emotion
And the response
Falls the Shadow
                    Life is very long

T. S. ELIOT

Between the desire

85 And the spasm

Between the potency

And the existence

Between the essence

And the descent

90 Falls the Shadow

For Thine is the Kingdom

For Thine is

Life is

For Thine is the

95 *This is the way the world ends*

This is the way the world ends

This is the way the world ends

Not with a bang but a whimper.

E. E. CUMMINGS

1894–1962

An early follower of the imagist movement, E. E. Cummings was a successful visual artist as well as a poet, and by the time he published his first book of poetry in 1923, his poems were meant to be looked at as well as read. During World War I, Cummings volunteered as an ambulance driver; he later abandoned the unit in Paris and was detained for three months on suspicion of espionage. *The Enormous Room* (1922) recounts this experience. Though seldom given credit for his influence on the Black Mountain and L=A=N=G=U=A=G=E movements of the late twentieth century, Cummings was their pioneer.

I am a small eye poet.

1. LIZ

with breathing as(faithfully)her lownecked
dress a little topples and slightly expands

one square foot mired in silk wrinkling loth
stocking begins queerly to do a few
5   gestures to death,
                the silent shoulders are both
slowly with pinkish ponderous arms bedecked
whose white thick wrists deliver promptly to
a deep lap enormous mindless hands.
10   and no one knows what(i am sure of this)
her blunt unslender,what her big unkeen

"Business is rotten"the face yawning said

what her mouth thinks of
                (if it were a kiss
15 distinct entirely melting sinuous lean...
whereof this lady in some book had read

because it's

Spring
thingS

dare to do people

5   (& not
the other way

round)because it

's A
pril

10   Lives lead their own

persons(in
stead

of everybodyelse's)but

what's wholly
15   marvellous my

Darling

is that you &
i are more than you

& i(be

20   ca
us

e It's we)

a great

man
is
gone.

5   Tall as the truth

was who:and
wore his(mountains
understand

how)life

10 like a(now
with
one sweet sun

in it,now with a

million
15 flaming billion kinds
of nameless

silence)sky;

who are you,little i

(five or six years old)
peering from some high

window;at the gold

5 of november sunset

(and feeling:that if day
has to become night

this is a beautiful way)

Buffalo Bill 's

defunct

    who used to

    ride a watersmooth-silver

                                stallion

and break onetwothreefourfive pigeonsjustlikethat

                                      Jesus

he was a handsome man

                   and what i want to know is

how do you like your blueeyed boy

Mister Death

if there are any heavens my mother will(all by herself)have
one.   It will not be a pansy heaven nor
a fragile heaven of lilies-of-the-valley but
it will be a heaven of blackred roses

5   my father will be(deep like a rose
tall like a rose)

standing near my

swaying over her
(silent)
10   with eyes which are really petals and see

nothing with the face of a poet really which
is a flower and not a face with
hands
which whisper
15   This is my beloved my

                 (suddenly in sunlight
he will bow,

& the whole garden will bow)

somewhere i have never travelled,gladly beyond
any experience,your eyes have their silence:
in your most frail gesture are things which enclose me,
or which i cannot touch because they are too near

5   your slightest look easily will unclose me
though i have closed myself as fingers,
you open always petal by petal myself as Spring opens
(touching skilfully,mysteriously)her first rose

or if your wish be to close me,i and
10   my life will shut very beautifully,suddenly,
as when the heart of this flower imagines
the snow carefully everywhere descending;

nothing which we are to perceive in this world equals
the power of your intense fragility:whose texture
15   compels me with the colour of its countries,
rendering death and forever with each breathing

(i do not know what it is about you that closes
and opens;only something in me understands
the voice of your eyes is deeper than all roses)
nobody,not even the rain,has such small hands

at dusk
     just when
the Light is filled with birds
seriously
5   i begin

to climb the best hill,
driven by black wine.
a village does not move
behind my eye

10   the windmills are
silent
their flattened arms
complain steadily against the west

one Clock dimly cries
15   nine,i stride among the vines
(my heart pursues
against the little moon

a here and there lark
                    who;rises,
20   and;droops
as if upon a thread invisible)

A graveyard dreams through its
cluttered and brittle emblems,or
a field(and i pause among
25   the smell of minute mown lives)oh

my spirit you
tumble
climb

     and mightily fatally

30   i remark how through deep lifted
fields Oxen distinctly move,a
yellowandbluish cat(perched why
Curvingly at this)window;yes

women sturdily meander in my
35   mind,woven by always upon
sunset,
crickets within me whisper

whose erect blood finally
trembles,emerging to perceive
40   buried in cliff
                precisely

at the Ending of this road,
a candle in a shrine:
its puniest flame persists
shaken by the sea

l(a

le
af
fa

5   ll

s)
one
l

iness

HART CRANE

1899–1932

Often compared to the French symbolists, particularly to Arthur Rimbaud, Hart Crane is considered a poet of extraordinary metaphor and visionary journey. He lived a frustrating life, trying to satisfy difficult parents and struggling to make a career out of writing poetry. Eventually he came to depend on the financial support of friends and patrons. His first book, *White Buildings* (1926), collects the shorter poems, but he aspired to a grand level of achievement, working for seven years on *The Bridge* (1930), a long poem of significant range and ambition. He did achieve some critical and financial success in his lifetime and knew many of his famous contemporaries, including E. E. Cummings and Allen Tate. In 1931, Crane sailed to Mexico, hoping to work on another long poem. On his return trip to New York on the *Orizaba,* he committed suicide by jumping overboard.

The problem of form becomes harder and harder for me every day. . . . One must be drenched in words, literally soaked with them to have the right ones form themselves into the proper pattern at the right moment.

As silent as a mirror is believed
Realities plunge in silence by . . .

I am not ready for repentance;
Nor to match regrets. For the moth
5   Bends no more than the still
Imploring flame. And tremorous
In the white falling flakes
Kisses are,—
The only worth all granting.

10   It is to be learned—
This cleaving and this burning,
But only by the one who
Spends out himself again.

Twice and twice
15   (Again the smoking souvenir,
Bleeding eidolon!) and yet again.
Until the bright logic is won
Unwhispering as a mirror
Is believed.

20   Then, drop by caustic drop, a perfect cry
Shall string some constant harmony,—
Relentless caper for all those who step
The legend of their youth into the noon.

There are no stars to-night
But those of memory.
Yet how much room for memory there is
In the loose girdle of soft rain.

5   There is even room enough
For the letters of my mother's mother,
Elizabeth,
That have been pressed so long
Into a corner of the roof
10   That they are brown and soft,
And liable to melt as snow.

Over the greatness of such space
Steps must be gentle.
It is all hung by an invisible white hair.
15   It trembles as birch limbs webbing the air.

And I ask myself:

"Are your fingers long enough to play
Old keys that are but echoes:
Is the silence strong enough
20   To carry back the music to its source
And back to you again
As though to her?"

Yet I would lead my grandmother by the hand
Through much of what she would not understand;
25   And so I stumble. And the rain continues on the roof
With such a sound of gently pitying laughter.

GARDEN ABSTRACT

The apple on its bough is her desire,—
Shining suspension, mimic of the sun.
The bough has caught her breath up, and her voice,
Dumbly articulate in the slant and rise
Of branch on branch above her, blurs her eyes.
She is prisoner of the tree and its green fingers.

And so she comes to dream herself the tree,
The wind possessing her, weaving her young veins,
Holding her to the sky and its quick blue,
Drowning the fever of her hands in sunlight.
She has no memory, nor fear, nor hope
Beyond the grass and shadows at her feet.

We make our meek adjustments,
Contented with such random consolations
As the wind deposits
In slithered and too ample pockets.

5 For we can still love the world, who find
A famished kitten on the step, and know
Recesses for it from the fury of the street,
Or warm torn elbow coverts.

We will sidestep, and to the final smirk
10 Dally the doom of that inevitable thumb
That slowly chafes its puckered index toward us,
Facing the dull squint with what innocence
And what surprise!

And yet these fine collapses are not lies
15 More than the pirouettes of any pliant cane;
Our obsequies are, in a way, no enterprise.
We can evade you, and all else but the heart:
What blame to us if the heart live on.

The game enforces smirks; but we have seen
20 The moon in lonely alleys make
A grail of laughter of an empty ash can,
And through all sound of gaiety and quest
Have heard a kitten in the wilderness.

Regard the capture here, O Janus-faced,
As double as the hands that twist this glass.
Such eyes at search or rest you cannot see;
Reciting pain or glee, how can you bear!

5 Twin shadowed halves: the breaking second holds
In each the skin alone, and so it is
I crust a plate of vibrant mercury
Borne cleft to you, and brother in the half.

Inquire this much-exacting fragment smile,
10 Its drums and darkest blowing leaves ignore,—
Defer though, revocation of the tears
That yield attendance to one crucial sign.

Look steadily—how the wind feasts and spins
The brain's disk shivered against lust. Then watch
15 While darkness, like an ape's face, falls away,
And gradually white buildings answer day.

Let the same nameless gulf beleaguer us—
Alike suspend us from atrocious sums
Built floor by floor on shafts of steel that grant
20 The plummet heart, like Absalom, no stream.

The highest tower,—let her ribs palisade
Wrenched gold of Nineveh;—yet leave the tower.
The bridge swings over salvage, beyond wharves;
A wind abides the ensign of your will . . .

25 In alternating bells have you not heard
All hours clapped dense into a single stride?
Forgive me for an echo of these things,
And let us walk through time with equal pride.

LANGSTON HUGHES

1902–1967

A central figure in the Harlem Renaissance, Langston Hughes was a prolific writer of poetry, novels, plays, short stories, newspaper columns, and essays. Hughes admired Paul Laurence Dunbar and Carl Sandburg, and he pursued a lifelong interest in jazz. Like Dunbar, he was criticized for his focus on the hardships of African American life. He spent many years abroad, including a year in the Soviet Union. Hughes's political views changed throughout his life, but in the early 1950s his career was almost derailed by the House Un-American Activities Committee. Joseph McCarthy and his committee were themselves discredited soon after, however, and Hughes continued to write, with varying critical acclaim, until his death.

I tried to write poems like the songs they sang on Seventh Street. . . . [Those songs] had the pulse beat of the people who keep on going.

I've known rivers:
I've known rivers ancient as the world and older than the
    flow of human blood in human veins.

My soul has grown deep like the rivers.

I bathed in the Euphrates when dawns were young.
I built my hut near the Congo and it lulled me to sleep.
I looked upon the Nile and raised the pyramids above it.
I heard the singing of the Mississippi when Abe Lincoln
    went down to New Orleans, and I've seen its muddy
    bosom turn all golden in the sunset.

I've known rivers:
Ancient, dusky rivers.

My soul has grown deep like the rivers.

I, too, sing America.

I am the darker brother.
They send me to eat in the kitchen
When company comes,
But I laugh,
And eat well,
And grow strong.

Tomorrow,
I'll be at the table
When company comes.
Nobody'll dare
Say to me,
"Eat in the kitchen,"
Then.

Besides,
They'll see how beautiful I am
And be ashamed—

I, too, am America.

Droning a drowsy syncopated tune,
Rocking back and forth to a mellow croon,
    I heard a Negro play.
Down on Lenox Avenue the other night
₅ By the pale dull pallor of an old gas light
      He did a lazy sway....
      He did a lazy sway....
To the tune o' those Weary Blues.
With his ebony hands on each ivory key
₁₀ He made that poor piano moan with melody.
      O Blues!
Swaying to and fro on his rickety stool
He played that sad raggy tune like a musical fool.
      Sweet Blues!
₁₅ Coming from a black man's soul.
      O Blues!
In a deep song voice with a melancholy tone
I heard that Negro sing, that old piano moan—
    "Ain't got nobody in all this world,
₂₀   Ain't got nobody but ma self
      I's gwine to quit ma frownin'
      And put ma troubles on the shelf."

Thump, thump, thump, went his foot on the floor.
He played a few chords then he sang some more—
25   "I got the Weary Blues
            And I can't be satisfied.
            Got the Weary Blues
            And can't be satisfied—
            I ain't happy no mo'
30   And I wish that I had died."
And far into the night he crooned that tune.
The stars went out and so did the moon.
The singer stopped playing and went to bed
While the Weary Blues echoed through his head.
He slept like a rock or a man that's dead.

Dusk dark
On Railroad Avenue.
Lights in the fish joints,
Lights in the pool rooms.
5   A box-car some train
Has forgotten
In the middle of the
Block.
A player piano,
10   A victrola.
     942
     Was the number.
A boy
Lounging on a corner.
15   A passing girl
With purple powdered skin.
     Laughter
     Suddenly
     Like a taut drum.
20   Laughter
     Suddenly
     Neither truth nor lie.
     Laughter
Hardening the dusk dark evening.
25   Laughter
Shaking the lights in the fish joints,
Rolling white balls in the pool rooms,
And leaving untouched the box-car
Some train has forgotten.

Harlem
Knows a song
Without a tune—
The rhythm's there:
5 But the melody's
Bare.

Harlem
Knows a night
Without a moon.
10   The stars
Are where?

The instructor said,

> *Go home and write*
> *a page tonight.*
> *And let that page come out of you—*
> 5 *Then, it will be true.*

I wonder if it's that simple?
I am twenty-two, colored, born in Winston-Salem.
I went to school there, then Durham, then here
to this college on the hill above Harlem.
10 I am the only colored student in my class.
The steps from the hill lead down into Harlem,
through a park, then I cross St. Nicholas,
Eighth Avenue, Seventh, and I come to the Y,
the Harlem Branch Y, where I take the elevator
15 up to my room, sit down, and write this page:

It's not easy to know what is true for you or me
at twenty-two, my age. But I guess I'm what
I feel and see and hear, Harlem, I hear you:
hear you, hear me—we two—you, me, talk on this page.
(I hear New York, too.) Me—who?
Well, I like to eat, sleep, drink, and be in love.
I like to work, read, learn, and understand life.
I like a pipe for a Christmas present,
or records—Bessie, bop, or Bach.
I guess being colored doesn't make me *not* like
the same things other folks like who are other races.
So will my page be colored that I write?
Being me, it will not be white.
But it will be
a part of you, instructor.
You are white—
yet a part of me, as I am a part of you.
That's American.
Sometimes perhaps you don't want to be a part of me.
Nor do I often want to be a part of you.
But we are, that's true!
As I learn from you,
I guess you learn from me—
although you're older—and white—
and somewhat more free.

This is my page for English B.

LANGSTON HUGHES

HARLEM [2]

What happens to a dream deferred?

    Does it dry up
    like a raisin in the sun?
    Or fester like a sore—
5   And then run?
    Does it stink like rotten meat?
    Or crust and sugar over
    like a syrupy sweet?

    Maybe it just sags
10   like a heavy load.

    Or does it explode?

THEODORE ROETHKE

1908–1963

Theodore Roethke grew up in Saginaw, Michigan, among the greenhouses his father and grandfather operated as the family business. His poetry often dwells on the relationship between father and son, and on the physical facts of the natural world. Roethke taught at the University of Washington and had a strong influence on poets of the American Northwest. Always attentive to the sound and rhythm of the poetic line, Roethke was less a formal poet than one with an instinctive grasp of the sound and structure of language.

You can't make poetry simply by avoiding clichés.

CHILD ON TOP OF A GREENHOUSE

The wind billowing out the seat of my britches,
My feet crackling splinters of glass and dried putty,
The half-gown chrysanthemums staring up like accusers,
Up through the streaked glass, flashing with sunlight,
5   A few white clouds all rushing eastward,
A line of elms plunging and tossing like horses,
And everyone, everyone pointing up and shouting!

I knew a woman, lovely in her bones,
When small birds sighed, she would sigh back at them;
Ah, when she moved, she moved more ways than one:
The shapes a bright container can contain!
5 Of her choice virtues only gods should speak,
Or English poets who grew up on Greek
(I'd have them sing in chorus, cheek to cheek).

How well her wishes went! She stroked my chin,
She taught me Turn, and Counter-turn, and Stand;
10 She taught me Touch, that undulant white skin;
I nibbled meekly from her proffered hand;
She was the sickle; I, poor I, the rake,
Coming behind her for her pretty sake
(But what prodigious mowing we did make).

15 Love likes a gander, and adores a goose:
Her full lips pursed, the errant note to seize;
She played it quick, she played it light and loose;
My eyes, they dazzled at her flowing knees;
Her several parts could keep a pure repose,
20 Or one hip quiver with a mobile nose
(She moved in circles, and those circles moved).

Let seed be grass, and grass turn into hay:
I'm martyr to a motion not my own;
What's freedom for? To know eternity.
25 I swear she cast a shadow white as stone.
But who would count eternity in days?
These old bones live to learn her wanton ways:
(I measure time by how a body sways).

THE VOICE

One feather is a bird,
I claim; one tree, a wood;
In her low voice I heard
More than a mortal should;
5   And so I stood apart,
Hidden in my own heart.

And yet I roamed out where
Those notes went, like the bird,
Whose thin song hung in air,
10   Diminished, yet still heard:
I lived with open sound,
Aloft, and on the ground.

That ghost was my own choice,
The shy cerulean bird;
15   It sang with her true voice,
And it was I who heard
A slight voice reply;
I heard; and only I.

Desire exults the ear:
20   Bird, girl, and ghostly tree,
The earth, the solid air—
Their slow song sang in me;
The long noon pulsed away,
Like any summer day.

I wake to sleep, and take my waking slow.
I feel my fate in what I cannot fear.
I learn by going where I have to go.

We think by feeling. What is there to know?
I hear my being dance from ear to ear.
I wake to sleep, and take my waking slow.

Of those so close beside me, which are you?
God bless the Ground! I shall walk softly there,
And learn by going where I have to go.

Light takes the Tree; but who can tell us how?
The lowly worm climbs up a winding stair;
I wake to sleep, and take my waking slow.

Great Nature has another thing to do
To you and me; so take the lively air,
And, lovely, learn by going where to go.

This shaking keeps me steady. I should know.
What falls away is always. And is near.
I wake to sleep, and take my waking slow.
I learn by going where I have to go.

1

A gull rides on the ripples of a dream,
White upon white, slow-settling on a stone;
Across my lawn the soft-backed creatures come;
In the weak light they wander, each alone.
5   Bring me the meek, for I would know their ways;
I am a connoisseur of midnight eyes.
The small! The small! I hear them singing clear
On the long banks, in the soft summer air.

2

What is there for the soul to understand?
10   The slack face of the dismal pure inane?
The wind dies down; my will dies with the wind,
God's in that stone, or I am not a man!
Body and soul transcend appearances
Before the caving-in of all that is;
15   I'm dying piecemeal, fervent in decay;
My moments linger—that's eternity.

3

A late rose ravages the casual eye,
A blaze of being on a central stem.
It lies upon us to undo the lie
20   Of living merely in the realm of time.
Existence moves toward a certain end—
A thing all earthly lovers understand.
That dove's elaborate way of coming near
Reminds me I am dying with the year.

4

25   A tree arises on a central plain—
It is no trick of change or chance of light.
A tree all out of shape from wind and rain,
A tree thinned by the wind obscures my sight.
The long day dies; I walked the woods alone;
30   Beyond the ridge two wood thrush sing as one.
Being delights in being, and in time.
The evening wraps me, steady as a flame.

THEODORE ROETHKE

1

A dark theme keeps me here,
Though summer blazes in the vireo's eye.
Who would be half possessed
By his own nakedness?
5   Waking's my care—
I'll make a broken music, or I'll die.

2

Ye littles, lie more close!
Make me, O Lord, a last, a simple thing
Time cannot overwhelm.
10   Once I transcended time:
A bud broke to a rose,
And I rose from a last diminishing.

3

I look down the far light
And I behold the dark side of a tree
15   Far down a billowing plain,
And when I look again,
It's lost upon the night—
Night I embrace, a dear proximity.

4

I stand by a low fire
20   Counting the wisps of flame, and I watch how
Light shifts upon the wall.
I bid stillness be still.
I see, in evening air,
How slowly dark comes down on what we do.

1

Was I too glib about eternal things,
An intimate of air and all its songs?
Pure aimlessness pursued and yet pursued
And all wild longings of the insatiate blood
Brought me down to my knees. O who can be
Both moth and flame? The weak moth blundering by.
Whom do we love? I thought I knew the truth;
Of grief I died, but no one knew my death.

2

I saw a body dancing in the wind,
A shape called up out of my natural mind;
I heard a bird stir in its true confine;
A nestling sighed—I called that nestling mine;
A partridge drummed; a minnow nudged its stone;
We danced, we danced, under a dancing moon;
And on the coming of the outrageous dawn,
We danced together, we danced on and on.

3

Morning's a motion in a happy mind:
She stayed in light, as leaves live in the wind,
Swaying in air, like some long water weed.
She left my body, lighter than a seed;
I gave her body full and grave farewell.
A wind came close, like a shy animal.
A light leaf on a tree, she swayed away
To the dark beginnings of another day.

25   Was nature kind? The heart's core tractable?
All waters waver, and all fires fail.
Leaves, leaves, lean forth and tell me what I am;
This single tree turns into purest flame.
I am a man, a man at intervals
30   Pacing a room, a room with dead-white walls;
I feel the autumn fail—all that slow fire
Denied in me, who has denied desire.

ELIZABETH BISHOP

1911–1979

After graduating from Vassar in 1934, Elizabeth Bishop traveled in Europe and North Africa. She lived in Rio de Janeiro for several years and, after returning to the United States, taught at the University of Washington and Harvard. She also served a term as consultant in poetry to the Library of Congress, a position now known as poet laureate. Often considered a formalist, Bishop finds beauty in the visceral details of nature, creating images that join the inner workings of life with the life of the mind. Her awards include the Pulitzer Prize, the National Book Award, and the Order of Rio Branco (Brazil).

I'm not interested in big-scale work as such.
Something needn't be large to be good.

Alone on the railroad track
    I walked with pounding heart.
The ties were too close together
    or maybe too far apart.

5   The scenery was impoverished:
    scrub-pine and oak; beyond
its mingled gray-green foliage
    I saw the little pond

where the dirty hermit lives,
10   lie like an old tear
holding onto its injuries
    lucidly year after year.

The hermit shot off his shot-gun
    and the tree by his cabin shook.
15   Over the pond went a ripple.
    The pet hen went chook-chook.

"Love should be put into action!"
    screamed the old hermit.
Across the pond an echo
    tried and tried to confirm it.

I caught a tremendous fish
and held him beside the boat
half out of water, with my hook
fast in a corner of his mouth.

5   He didn't fight.
He hadn't fought at all.
He hung a grunting weight,
battered and venerable
and homely. Here and there

10   his brown skin hung in strips
like ancient wallpaper,
and its pattern of darker brown
was like wallpaper:
shapes like full-blown roses

15   stained and lost through age.
He was speckled with barnacles,
fine rosettes of lime,
and infested
with tiny white sea-lice,

20   and underneath two or three
rags of green weed hung down.
While his gills were breathing in
the terrible oxygen
—the frightening gills,

25   fresh and crisp with blood,
that can cut so badly—
I thought of the coarse white flesh
packed in like feathers,
the big bones and the little bones,

30   the dramatic reds and blacks
of his shiny entrails,
and the pink swim-bladder

like a big peony.
I looked into his eyes
35 which were far larger than mine
but shallower, and yellowed,
the irises backed and packed
with tarnished tinfoil
seen through the lenses
40 of old scratched isinglass.
They shifted a little, but not
to return my stare.
—It was more like the tipping
of an object toward the light.
45 I admired his sullen face,
the mechanism of his jaw,
and then I saw
that from his lower lip
—if you could call it a lip—
50 grim, wet, and weaponlike,
hung five old pieces of fish-line,
or four and a wire leader
with the swivel still attached,
with all their five big hooks
55 grown firmly in his mouth.
A green line, frayed at the end
where he broke it, two heavier lines,
and a fine black thread
still crimped from the strain and snap
60 when it broke and he got away.
Like medals with their ribbons
frayed and wavering,
a five-haired beard of wisdom
trailing from his aching jaw.

65   I stared and stared
and victory filled up
the little rented boat,
from the pool of bilge
where oil had spread a rainbow
70   around the rusted engine
to the bailer rusted orange,
the sun-cracked thwarts,
the oarlocks on their strings,
the gunnels—until everything
75   was rainbow, rainbow, rainbow!
And I let the fish go.

ELIZABETH BISHOP

From Brooklyn, over the Brooklyn Bridge, on this fine morning,
    please come flying.
In a cloud of fiery pale chemicals,
    please come flying,
to the rapid rolling of thousands of small blue drums
descending out of the mackerel sky
over the glittering grandstand of harbor-water,
    please come flying.

Whistles, pennants and smoke are blowing. The ships
are signaling cordially with multitudes of flags
rising and falling like birds all over the harbor.
Enter: two rivers, gracefully bearing
countless little pellucid jellies
in cut-glass epergnes dragging with silver chains.
The flight is safe; the weather is all arranged.
The waves are running in verses this fine morning.
    Please come flying.

Come with the pointed toe of each black shoe
trailing a sapphire highlight,
with a black capeful of butterfly wings and bon-mots,
with heaven knows how many angels all riding
on the broad black brim of your hat,
    please come flying.

Bearing a musical inaudible abacus,
a slight censorious frown, and blue ribbons,
    please come flying.
Facts and skyscrapers glint in the tide; Manhattan
is all awash with morals this fine morning,
    so please come flying.

30   Mounting the sky with natural heroism,
    above the accidents, above the malignant movies,
    the taxicabs and injustices at large,
    while horns are resounding in your beautiful ears
    that simultaneously listen to
35   a soft uninvented music, fit for the musk deer,
          please come flying.

    For whom the grim museums will behave
    like courteous male bower-birds,
    for whom the agreeable lions lie in wait
40   on the steps of the Public Library,
    eager to rise and follow through the doors
    up into the reading rooms,
          please come flying.
    We can sit down and weep; we can go shopping,
45   or play at a game of constantly being wrong
    with a priceless set of vocabularies,
    or we can bravely deplore, but please
          please come flying.

    With dynasties of negative constructions
50   darkening and dying around you,
    with grammar that suddenly turns and shines
    like flocks of sandpipers flying,
          please come flying.

    Come like a light in the white mackerel sky,
55   come like a daytime comet
    with a long unnebulous train of words,
    from Brooklyn, over the Brooklyn Bridge, on this fine morning,
          please come flying.

ELIZABETH BISHOP

September rain falls on the house.
In the failing light, the old grandmother
sits in the kitchen with the child
beside the Little Marvel Stove,
5   reading the jokes from the almanac,
laughing and talking to hide her tears.

She thinks that her equinoctial tears
and the rain that beats on the roof of the house
were both foretold by the almanac,
10   but only known to a grandmother.
The iron kettle sings on the stove.
She cuts some bread and says to the child,

It's time for tea now; but the child
is watching the teakettle's small hard tears
15   dance like mad on the hot black stove,
the way the rain must dance on the house.
Tidying up, the old grandmother
hangs up the clever almanac

on its string. Birdlike, the almanac
20   hovers half open above the child,
hovers above the old grandmother
and her teacup full of dark brown tears.
She shivers and says she thinks the house
feels chilly, and puts more wood in the stove.

25   *It was to be,* says the Marvel Stove.
I know what I know, says the almanac.
With crayons the child draws a rigid house
and a winding pathway. Then the child
puts in a man with buttons like tears
30   and shows it proudly to the grandmother.

But secretly, while the grandmother
busies herself about the stove,
the little moons fall down like tears
from between the pages of the almanac
35   into the flower bed the child
has carefully placed in the front of the house.

Time to plant tears, says the almanac.
The grandmother sings to the marvellous stove
and the child draws another inscrutable house.

INSOMNIA

The moon in the bureau mirror
looks out a million miles
(and perhaps with pride, at herself,
but she never, never smiles)
far and away beyond sleep, or
perhaps she's a daytime sleeper.

By the Universe deserted,
she'd tell it to go to hell,
and she'd find a body of water,
or a mirror, on which to dwell.
So wrap up care in a cobweb
and drop it down the well

into that world inverted
where left is always right,
where the shadows are really the body,
where we stay awake all night,
where the heavens are shallow as the sea
is now deep, and you love me.

The roaring alongside he takes for granted,
and that every so often the world is bound to shake.
He runs, he runs to the south, finical, awkward,
in a state of controlled panic, a student of Blake.

5　The beach hisses like fat. On his left, a sheet
of interrupting water comes and goes
and glazes over his dark and brittle feet.
He runs, he runs straight through it, watching his toes.

—Watching, rather, the spaces of sand between them,
10　where (no detail too small) the Atlantic drains
rapidly backwards and downwards. As he runs,
he stares at the dragging grains.

The world is a mist. And then the world is
minute and vast and clear. The tide
15　is higher or lower. He couldn't tell you which.
His beak is focussed; he is preoccupied,

looking for something, something, something.
Poor bird, he is obsessed!
The millions of grains are black, white, tan, and gray,
mixed with quartz grains, rose and amethyst.

IN MEMORIAM: ROBERT LOWELL

I can make out the rigging of a schooner
a mile off; I can count
the new cones on the spruce. It is so still
the pale bay wears a milky skin, the sky
5   *no clouds, except for one long, carded horse's-tail.*

The islands haven't shifted since last summer,
even if I like to pretend they have
—drifting, in a dreamy sort of way,
a little north, a little south or sidewise,
10   and that they're free within the blue frontiers of bay.

This month, our favorite one is full of flowers:
Buttercups, Red Clover, Purple Vetch,
Hawkweed still burning, Daisies pied, Eyebright,
the Fragrant Bedstraw's incandescent stars,
15   and more, returned, to paint the meadows with delight.

The Goldfinches are back, or others like them,
and the White-throated Sparrow's five-note song,
pleading and pleading, brings tears to the eyes.
Nature repeats herself, or almost does:
20   *repeat, repeat, repeat; revise, revise, revise.*

Years ago, you told me it was here
(in 1932?) you first "discovered *girls*"
and learned to sail, and learned to kiss.
You had "such fun," you said, that classic summer.
25   ("Fun"—it always seemed to leave you at a loss . . .)

You left North Haven, anchored in its rock,
afloat in mystic blue . . . And now—you've left
for good. You can't derange, or re-arrange,
your poems again. (But the Sparrows can their song.)
The words won't change again. Sad friend, you cannot change.

ROBERT HAYDEN

1913–1980

Born Asa Bundy Sheffey in Detroit, Robert Hayden was raised by both his mother and a foster family, the Haydens. He received degrees from Detroit City College (now Wayne State University) and the University of Michigan. He taught for more than twenty years at Fisk University, then returned to the University of Michigan as a professor of English. In both his politics and his poetry, Hayden expressed a deep belief in the unity of humanity beyond racial identity. He was awarded the grand prize for poetry at the First World Festival of Negro Arts in Senegal, and he also became the first African American consultant in poetry to the Library of Congress. Despite these achievements, Hayden was frequently criticized by other African American artists for his insistence that he be known as an American poet, not an "Afro-American" poet.

One cannot learn to be a poet. One is born a poet. One does not choose this art but is chosen by it. And, finally, it is a gift, something given, and if you are to be worthy to receive it you must give everything you are in return.

FOR ROSEY

Her parents and her dolls destroyed,
   her childhood foreclosed,
she watched the foreign soldiers from
   the sunlit window whose black bars

5   Were crooked crosses inked upon
   her pallid face. "Liebchen,
Liebchen, you should be in bed."
   But she felt ill no longer.

And because that day was a holy day
10   when even the dead, it seemed,
must rise, she was allowed to stay
   and see the golden strangers who

Were Father, Brother, and her dream
   of God. Afterwards
15   she said, "They were so beautiful,
   and they were not afraid."

Sundays too my father got up early
and put his clothes on in the blueblack cold,
then with cracked hands that ached
from labor in the weekday weather made
5   banked fires blaze. No one ever thanked him.

I'd wake and hear the cold splintering, breaking.
When the rooms were warm, he'd call,
and slowly I would rise and dress,
fearing the chronic angers of that house.

10 Speaking indifferently to him,
who had driven out the cold
and polished my good shoes as well.
What did I know, what did I know
of love's austere and lonely offices?

Sprawled in the pigsty,
    snouts nudging snuffling him—
a naked old man
    with bloodstained wings.

5   Fallen from the August sky?
Dead? Alive?
    But he twists away

from the cattle-prod, wings
    jerking, lifts his grizzled head,
10 regarding all
    with searching eyes.

Neither smiles nor threats,
dumbshow nor lingua franca
were of any use to those
15 trying for clues to him.

They could not make him hide
his nakedness
in their faded hand-me-downs.

Humane, if hostile and afraid,
20 they spread him a pallet
in the chicken-house.
The rooster pecked his wings.

Leftovers were set out for him;
he ate sunflowers
25 instead and the lice crawling his feathers.

Carloads of the curious paid
his clever hosts to see the
actual angel? carny freak?
in the barbedwire pen.

30 They crossed themselves and prayed
his blessing;
catcalled and chunked at him.

In the dark his heavy wings
open and shut, stiffly spread
35   like a wooden butterfly's.

He leaps, board wings clum-
sily flapping, big sex
flopping, falls.

The hawk-hunted fowl
40 flutter and squawk;
panic squeals in the sty.

He strains, an awk-
ward patsy, sweating strains
leaping falling. Then—

45   silken rustling in the air,
the angle of ascent
achieved.

FOR STEVE AND NANCY, ALLEN AND MAGDA

Always this waking dream of palmtrees,
magic flowers—of sensual joys
like treasures brought up from the sea.

Always this longing, this nostalgia
5   for tropic islands we
have never known and yet recall.

We look for ease upon these islands named
to honor holiness; in their chromatic
torpor catch our breath.

10   Scorn greets us with promises of rum,
hostility welcomes us to bargain sales.
We make friends with Flamboyant trees.

Jamaican Cynthie, called alien by dese lazy
islanders—wo'k hahd, treated bad,
15   oh, mahn, I tellin you. She's full

of raucous anger. Nevertheless brings gifts of
scarlet hibiscus when she comes to clean,
white fragrant spider-lilies too sometimes.

The roofless walls, the tidy ruins
20   of a sugar mill. More than cane
was crushed. But I am tired today

of history, its patina'd cliches
of endless evil. Flame trees.
The intricate sheen of waters flowing into sun.

25 I wake and see
the morning like a god
in peacock-flower mantle dancing

on opalescent waves—
and can believe my furies have
abandoned for a time their long pursuit.

ROBERT HAYDEN

RANDALL JARRELL

1914–1965

In his lifetime, Randall Jarrell was known as much for his literary criticism as for his verse; his essays on poets and poetry helped to build the careers of Robert Lowell, Elizabeth Bishop, and William Carlos Williams, among others. Today he is remembered for the often stark and understated poems that capture his experiences as a soldier in World War II. In 1965, having recently attempted suicide and suffering from depression, Jarrell was struck by a car and killed; whether or not his death was accidental remains a point of controversy.

The real war poets are always war poets, peace or any time.

At home, in my flannel gown, like a bear to its floe,
I clambered to bed; up the globe's impossible sides
I sailed all night—till at last, with my black beard,
My furs and my dogs, I stood at the northern pole.

5   There in the childish night my companions lay frozen,
The stiff furs knocked at my starveling throat,
And I gave my great sigh: the flakes came huddling,
Were they really my end? In the darkness I turned to my rest.

—Here, the flag snaps in the glare and silence
10   Of the unbroken ice. I stand here,
The dogs bark, my beard is black, and I stare
At the North Pole . . .
               And now what? Why, go back.

Turn as I please, my step is to the south.
15   The world—my world spins on this final point
Of cold and wretchedness: all lines, all winds
End in this whirlpool I at last discover.

And it is meaningless. In the child's bed
After the night's voyage, in that warm world
20   Where people work and suffer for the end
That crowns the pain—in that Cloud-Cuckoo-Land

I reached my North and it had meaning.
Here at the actual pole of my existence,
Where all that I have done is meaningless,
25   Where I die or live by accident alone—

Where, living or dying, I am still alone;
Here where North, the night, the berg of death
Crowd me out of the ignorant darkness,
I see at last that all the knowledge

30   I wrung from the darkness—that the darkness flung me—
Is worthless as ignorance: nothing comes from nothing,
The darkness from the darkness. Pain comes from the darkness
And we call it wisdom. It is pain.

THE DEATH OF THE BALL TURRET GUNNER

From my mother's sleep I fell into the State,
And I hunched in its belly till my wet fur froze.
Six miles from earth, loosed from its dream of life,
I woke to black flak and the nightmare fighters.
When I died they washed me out of the turret with a hose.

When I was home last Christmas
I called on your family,
Your aunts and your mother, your sister;
They were kind as ever to me.

5   They told me how well I was looking
And clearly admired my wife;
I drank tea, made conversation,
And played with my bread, or knife.

Your aunts seemed greyer; your mother's
10   Lame unexpecting smile
Wandered from doily to doily;
Your dead face still

Cast me, with parted lips,
Its tight-rope-walker's look. . . .
15   But who is there now to notice
If I look or do not look

At a photograph at your mother's?
There is no one left to care
For all we said, and did, and thought—
The world we were.

The saris go by me from the embassies.

Cloth from the moon. Cloth from another planet.
They look back at the leopard like the leopard.

And I. . . .
5   this print of mine, that has kept its color
Alive through so many cleanings; this dull null
Navy I wear to work, and wear from work, and so
To my bed, so to my grave, with no
Complaints, no comment: neither from my chief,
10 The Deputy Chief Assistant, nor his chief—
Only I complain. . . . this serviceable
Body that no sunlight dyes, no hand suffuses
But, dome-shadowed, withering among columns,
Wavy beneath fountains—small, far-off, shining
15 In the eyes of animals, these beings trapped
As I am trapped but not, themselves, the trap,
Aging, but without knowledge of their age,
Kept safe here, knowing not of death, for death—
Oh, bars of my own body, open, open!

20 The world goes by my cage and never sees me.
And there come not to me, as come to these,
The wild beasts, sparrows pecking the llamas' grain,
Pigeons settling on the bears' bread, buzzards
Tearing the meat the flies have clouded....

25   Vulture,
When you come for the white rat that the foxes left,
Take off the red helmet of your head, the black
Wings that have shadowed me, and step to me as man:
The wild brother at whose feet the white wolves fawn,
30 To whose hand of power the great lioness
Stalks, purring....

                         You know what I was,
You see what I am: change me, change me!

I ate pancakes one night in a Pancake House
Run by a lady my age. She was gay.
When I told her that I came from Pasadena
She laughed and said, "I lived in Pasadena
When Fatty Arbuckle drove the El Molino bus."

I felt that I had met someone from home.
No, not Pasadena, Fatty Arbuckle.
Who's that? Oh, something that we had in common
Like—like—the false armistice. Piano rolls.
She told me her house was the first Pancake House

East of the Mississippi, and I showed her
A picture of my grandson. Going home—
Home to the hotel—I began to hum,
"Smile a while, I bid you sad adieu,
When the clouds roll back I'll come to you."

Let's brush our hair before we go to bed,
I say to the old friend who lives in my mirror.
I remember how I'd brush my mother's hair
Before she bobbed it. How long has it been
Since I hit my funnybone? had a scab on my knee?

Here are Mother and Father in a photograph,
Father's holding me. . . . They both look so *young*.
I'm so much older than they are. Look at them,
Two babies with their baby. I don't blame you,
You weren't old enough to know any better;

If I could I'd go back, sit down by you both,
And sign our true armistice: you weren't to blame.
I shut my eyes and there's our living room.
The piano's playing something by Chopin,
30 And Mother and Father and their little girl

Listen. Look, the keys go down by themselves!
I go over, hold my hands out, play I play—
If only, somehow, I had learned to live!
The three of us sit watching, as my waltz
Plays itself out a half-inch from my fingers.

WILLIAM STAFFORD

1914–1993

Following the example of William Carlos Williams, William Stafford wrote with an ear for everyday speech. A conscientious objector during World War II and a supporter of pacifist organizations, Stafford worked in civilian public service camps during the war and chronicled these experiences in his memoir *Down My Heart*. He devoted much of his life to teaching and was a member of the faculty at Lewis and Clark College in Portland, Oregon, for more than thirty years. He published his first book of poems, *West of Your City,* at age forty-six. Stafford served as consultant in poetry to the Library of Congress, and his many honors include the National Book Award. Although he did not publish until middle age, he was prolific, producing more than sixty books of poetry and prose.

I get up at an early hour and the day's work in poetry-writing is done so inconspicuously that they [his family] don't even know it happens.

Traveling through the dark I found a deer
dead on the edge of the Wilson River road.
It is usually best to roll them into the canyon:
that road is narrow; to swerve might make more dead.

5   By glow of the tail-light I stumbled back of the car
and stood by the heap, a doe, a recent killing;
she had stiffened already, almost cold.
I dragged her off; she was large in the belly.

My fingers touching her side brought me the reason—
10 her side was warm; her fawn lay there waiting,
alive, still, never to be born.
Beside that mountain road I hesitated.

The car aimed ahead its lowered parking lights;
under the hood purred the steady engine.
15 I stood in the glare of the warm exhaust turning red;
around our group I could hear the wilderness listen.

I thought hard for us all—my only swerving—,
then pushed her over the edge into the river.

My father's gravestone said, "I knew it was time."
Our house was alive. It moved,
it had a song. The singers back home
all stood in rows along the railroad line.

5   When the wind came along the track
every neighbor sang. In the last
house I followed the wind—it
left the world and went on.

We knew, the wind and I, that space
10   ahead of us, the world like an empty room.
I looked back where the sky came down.
Some days no train would come.

Some birds didn't have a song.

WHAT GETS AWAY

Little things hide. Sometimes they
scuttle away like dry leaves in a sudden
wind. Tidepools are full of these
panicky creatures, and rock slides
have jittery populations hidden from the world
and even from each other.

Herodotus tells about the shyest
animal there is. It's the one even
Alexander the Great and his whole
conquering army had never seen, and people
—no matter how hard they try—
will never see.

The light along the hills in the morning
comes down slowly, naming the trees
white, then coasting the ground for stones to nominate.

Notice what this poem is not doing.

5   A house, a house, a barn, the old
quarry, where the river shrugs—
how much of this place is yours?

Notice what this poem is not doing.

Every person gone has taken a stone
10   to hold, and catch the sun. The carving
says, "Not here, but called away."

Notice what this poem is not doing.

The sun, the earth, the sky, all wait.
The crows and redbirds talk. The light
15   along the hills has come, has found you.

Notice what this poem has not done.

If we see better through tiny,
grim glasses, we like to wear
tiny, grim glasses.
Our parents willed us this
5   view. It's tundra? We love it.

We travel our kind of
Renaissance: barnfuls of hay,
whole voyages of corn, and
a book that flickers its
10   halo in the parlor.

Poverty plus confidence equals
pioneers. We never doubted.

GWENDOLYN BROOKS

1917–2000

Although born in Kansas, Gwendolyn Brooks was a poet of Chicago, the city she lived in and wrote about for most of her life. She published her first poem when she was thirteen years old; soon after, she met Langston Hughes, who encouraged her in her aspirations. In 1950, she became the first African American to win a Pulitzer Prize. Brooks stands out as one of the most visible poets of her time, not only publishing prodigiously but also participating in classes and contests aimed at improving the education of inner-city children.

Hear talk in the street. There is much real poetry coming out of the mouths of people in the street. Many clichés, yes, but also vitality and colorful strengths.

I think it must be lonely to be God.
Nobody loves a master. No. Despite
The bright hosannas, bright dear-Lords, and bright
Determined reverence of Sunday eyes.

5   Picture Jehovah striding through the hall
Of His importance, creatures running out
From servant-corners to acclaim, to shout
Appreciation of His merit's glare.

But who walks with Him?—dares to take His arm,
10   To slap Him on the shoulder, tweak His ear,
Buy Him a Coca-Cola or a beer,
Pooh-pooh His politics, call Him a fool?

Perhaps—who knows?—He tires of looking down.
Those eyes are never lifted. Never straight.
15   Perhaps sometimes He tires of being great
In solitude. Without a hand to hold.

Oh mother, mother, where is happiness?
They took my lover's tallness off to war.
Left me lamenting. Now I cannot guess
What I can use an empty heart-cup for.
He won't be coming back here any more.
Some day the war will end, but, oh, I knew
When he went walking grandly out that door
That my sweet love would have to be untrue.
Would have to be untrue. Would have to court
Coquettish death, whose impudent and strange
Possessive arms and beauty (of a sort)
Can make a hard man hesitate—and change.
And he will be the one to stammer, "Yes."
Oh mother, mother, where is happiness?

THE POOL PLAYERS.
SEVEN AT THE GOLDEN SHOVEL.

We real cool. We
Left school. We

Lurk late. We
Strike straight. We

5   Sing sin. We
Thin gin. We

Jazz June. We
Die soon.

Sisters,
where there is cold silence—
no hallelujahs, no hurrahs at all, no handshakes,
no neon red or blue, no smiling faces—
prevail.
Prevail across the editors of the world!
who are obsessed, self-honeying and self-crowned
in the seduced arena.

It has been a
hard trudge, with fainting, bandaging and death.
There have been startling confrontations.
There have been tramplings. Tramplings
of monarchs and of other men.

But there remain large countries in your eyes.
Shrewd sun.
The civil balance.
The listening secrets.

And you create and train your flowers still.

DENISE LEVERTOV

1923–1997

Born in England, Denise Levertov came to America with her husband in 1948 and became a naturalized citizen in 1956. Her father was a Hasidic Jew, but by the time Levertov was born he had converted to Christianity and had become an Anglican parson. Levertov was a child prodigy; entirely homeschooled, she corresponded with T. S. Eliot when she was twelve, published her first poem at seventeen, and published her first book at twenty-two. After arriving in America, she developed close literary friendships with William Carlos Williams and Robert Creeley. Levertov experimented with many forms and techniques in poetry and contributed a significant book of essays, *The Poet in the World* (1973), to the development of contemporary poetics.

One has to have a good ear, but you also have to read what you're working on aloud. Even if you have a good inner ear there are certain awkwardnesses that only become apparent when you speak out loud.

THE LOVERS

She: Since you have made me beautiful
    I am afraid
               not to be beautiful.
    The silvery dark mirror
5   looks past me: I
    cannot accept its silence
    the silence of your
    absence. I want
    my love for you to
10   shine from my eyes and hair
              till all the world wonders
    at the light your love has made.

He: At night, waking alone,
    I see you as if in a clear light
15   a flower held in the
    teeth of the dark.
    The mirror caught in its solitude
    cannot believe you as I believe.

"He with whom I ran hand in hand
kicking the leathery leaves down Oak Hill Path
thirty years ago,

appeared before me with anxious face, pale,
5   almost unrecognized, hesitant,
lame.

He whom I cannot remember hearing laugh out loud
but see in mind's eye smiling, self-approving,
wept on my shoulder.

10   He who seemed always
to take and not give, who took me
so long to forget,

remembered everything I had so long forgotten."

My wedding-ring lies in a basket
as if at the bottom of a well.
Nothing will come to fish it back up
and onto my finger again.
                              It lies
among keys to abandoned houses,
nails waiting to be needed and hammered
into some wall,
telephone numbers with no names attached,
idle paperclips.
                    It can't be given away
for fear of bringing ill-luck.
                    It can't be sold
for the marriage was good in its own
time, though that time is gone.
                    Could some artificer
beat into it bright stones, transform it
into a dazzling circlet no one could take
for solemn betrothal or to make promises
living will not let them keep? Change it
into a simple gift I could give in friendship?

They want to be their own old vision
of Mom and Dad. They want their dying son
to be eight years old again, not a gay man,
not ill, not dying. They have accepted him,
5   they would say if asked, unlike some who shut
errant sons out of house and heart,
and this makes them preen a little, secretly;
but enough of that, some voice within them
whispers, even more secretly, *he's our kid,*
10   *Mom and Dad are going to give him*
what all kids long for, a trip to Disney World,
what fun, the best Xmas ever.
And he, his wheelchair strung with bottles and tubes,
glass and metal glittering in winter sun,
15   shivers and sweats and tries to breathe as *Jingle Bells*
pervades the air and his mother, his father,
chatter and still won't talk, won't listen,
will never listen, never give him
the healing silence
20   in which they could have heard
his questions, his answers,
his life at last.

THE BATTERERS

A man sits by the bed
of a woman he has beaten,
dresses her wounds,
gingerly dabs at bruises.
5 Her blood pools about her,
darkens.

Astonished, he finds he's begun
to cherish her. He is terrified.
Why had he never
10 seen, before, what she was?
What if she stops breathing?

Earth, can we not love you
unless we believe the end is near?
Believe in your life
unless we think you are dying?

JOHN LOGAN

1923–1987

John Logan took an early interest in science, earning a bachelor's degree in zoology from Coe College. In graduate school, he shifted his attention to literature and philosophy. Logan returned often in his work to images of personal loss and the difficulties of family life. He attributed his reading style to the influence of E. E. Cummings, an early mentor; the musical qualities of Logan's language show the influence of Hart Crane and Dylan Thomas. Logan taught at many colleges and universities and was a legendary teacher and supporter of young poets. He published thirteen books of poetry, as well as an autobiographical novel, essays, and reviews. He served as poetry editor for *The Nation;* with photographer Aaron Siskind, he founded and edited *Choice,* a magazine of poetry and photography.

Poetry is an anonymous reaching out, which occasionally becomes personal—when there are those present who care to listen.

I was born on a street named Joy
of which I remember nothing,
but since I was a boy
I've looked for its lost turning.
5   Still I seem to hear my mother's cry
echo in the street of joy.
She was sick as Ruth for home
when I was born. My birth
took away my father's wife
10   and left me half
my life. Christ will my remorse
be less when my father's dead?
Or more. As Lincoln's minister of war
kept the body of his infant boy
15   in a silver coffin on his desk,
so I keep
in a small heirloom box of teak
the picture of my living father.
Or perhaps it is an image of myself
20   dead in this box she held?
I know her milk like ivory blood
still runs in my thick veins
and leaves in me an almost
lickerish taste for ghosts:
25   my mother's wan face,
full brown hair, the mammoth breast
death cuts off at the bone—
to which she draws her bow
again, brazen Amazon,
30   and aiming deadly as a saint
shoots her barb
of guilt into my game heart.

JANUARY 23, 1961

"I care more about strawberries than about death."
"Herr: es ist Zeit."

1

Lord, it is time now. The winter

has gone on and gone on.

Spring was brief.

Summer blasts the roots of trees and weeds

5   again, and you are dead

almost a year. I am sorry for my fear,

but you were father's age, and you were fond;

I saw it in your eyes when I put you on the plane.

Today it is too late to write

10   or visit as you asked.

I feel I let you die.

I chose the guilt over all the joy.

Now I know you cannot hear me say,

and so my elegy is for me.

2

15   I knew your serenity. Compassion.

Integrity. But I could not feel your death

until I visited your wife.

She is haggard with the burden of your loss.

I wish I had not come

20   before, when you were there,

and she served currant jam

on toast and you poured brandy in the tea

and laughed, slapping your thigh

and hopped, like a small, happy boy,

25 about your newly painted Village place.
    Now the color on your walls and hers
    is not fresh. It has peeled with the falling
    of your flesh. Your paintings in the house already date,
    especially the soft, romantic nude you did
30 (although I love it best):
    Her dark hair full to hips,
    girlish, unsucked breasts,
    rather pensive belly, skin
    a lucid gold or red like a faded blush.
35 Her beautiful, jet feminine bush.
    And the limbs you made, thin with their own light,
    with the glow of that other world:
    Women. Estlin, your poems are full of love—
    you wanted to know that other world
40 while you were still alive.
    All poets do. All men. All gods.
    Inside a woman we search for the lost wealth
    of our self. Marcel says,
    "Death is not a problem to be solved.
45 It is a mystery to be entered into."
    Then you have what you wanted, Estlin,
    for Death is a woman,
    and there is no more need for a poem.
    Your death fulfills and it is strong.
50 I wish I had not died when I was so young.

3

Your last summer at your farm
like a young man again you cut down
an aging, great New England oak.
Oh you are big and you would not start to stoop
55   even on that absolute day.
I feel you are a giant, tender gnome.
Like a child you came home
tired, and you called your wife
asking to be clean. Still tall you tossed
60   the odd body of your sweaty clothes
to her down, down the ancient stairs,
and it was there as the ghost
tumbled, suddenly you were struck
brilliant to your knees! Your back
65   bent. You wrapped your lean,
linen arms close around your life
naked as before our birth,
and began to weave away from earth
uttering with a huge, awkward, torn cry
the terrible, final poetry.

JULY 1963–AUGUST 1964

Blue's my older brother's color. Mine is brown, you see.
So today I bought this ring
of gold and lapis lazuli flecked with a bright bronze.
His blue is the light hue of his eyes. Brown's the color
5   of our dead mother's long hair,
which fell so beautifully about her young shoulders
in the picture, and of my own eyes (I can't tell hers).
I loved my brother, but never quite knew what to think.
For example, he would beat
10   me up as soon as the folks
left the house, and I would cry big, loud feminine tears.
He was good at sports and played football, and so instead
I was in the marching band.
My brother stole rubbers from the store and smoked cigars
15   and pipes, which made me sick. But
once we swam together in
the Nishnabotna River
near home, naked, our blue overalls piled together
by the water, their copper
20   buttons like the bronze glints in my ring. I remember
once when I was very young
I looked deep into a pool
of blue water—we had no mirror—and I was so
amazed I looked over my shoulder, for I did not
25   imagine it was me, caught
in that cerulean sky.
Thinking it was someone other, I tell you I con-
fused myself with my brother!
Nothing goes with gold, but I can see in this rich blue
30   stone the meeting of our clothes like the touching of hands
when he taught me to hold my fishing pole well and wound

up the reel for me. You know,
blue is the last of the primary colors to be named.
Why, some primitive societies still have no word
for it except "dark." It's associated with black:
in the night my brother and I
would play at games that neither of us could understand.
But this is not a confession; it is a question.
We've moved apart and don't write,
and our children don't even know their own cousin!
So, I would have you know I
want this ring to *engage* us
in reconciliation.
Blue is the color of the heart.
I won't live forever. Is it too late now to be
a brother to my brother?
Let the golden snake bend round
again to touch itself and
all at once burst into azure!

1974

There is a two-headed goat, a four-winged chicken
and a sad lamb with seven legs
whose complicated little life was spent in Hopland,
California. I saw the man with doubled eyes
5 who seemed to watch in me my doubts about my spirit.
Will it snag upon this aging flesh?

There is a strawberry that grew
out of a carrot plant, a blade
of grass that lanced through a thick rock,
10 a cornstalk nineteen-feet-two-inches tall grown by George
Osborne of Silome, Arkansas.
There is something grotesque growing in me I cannot tell.

It has been waxing, burgeoning, for a long time.
It weighs me down like the chains of the man of Lahore
15 who began collecting links on his naked body
until he crawled around the town carrying the last
thirteen years of his life six-hundred-seventy pounds.
Each link or each lump in me is an offense against love.

I want my own lit candle lamp buried in my skull
20 like the Lighthouse Man of Chungking,
who could lead the travelers home.
Well, I am still a traveler and I don't know where
I live. If my home is here, inside my breast,
light it up! And I will invite you in as my first guest.

FOR TINA LOGAN
AFTER VISITING THE BELIEVE IT OR NOT MUSEUM
WITH HER IN SAN FRANCISCO—1980

DONALD JUSTICE

1925–

Donald Justice studied with Robert Lowell and John Berryman while working on his doctorate at the University of Iowa. At first glance, Justice's poems may seem similar to Lowell's confessional works, but Justice's first-person narrator is frequently a persona, not himself. The author of several books of poems and essays, he has won both the Pulitzer Prize and the Bollingen Prize.

I've always felt it was the author's privilege to leave himself out if he chose—and I chose, contrary to the choice of certain friends and contemporaries.

TIME AND THE WEATHER

Time and the weather wear away
The houses that our fathers built.
Their ghostly furniture remains—
All the sad sofas we have stained
5   With tears of boredom or of guilt,

The fraying mottoes, the stopped clocks . . .
And still sometimes these tired shapes
Haunt the damp parlors of the heart.
What Sunday prisons they recall!
And what miraculous escapes!

Men at forty
Learn to close softly
The doors to rooms they will not be
Coming back to.

5 At rest on a stair landing,
They feel it moving
Beneath them now like the deck of a ship,
Though the swell is gentle.

And deep in mirrors
10 They rediscover
The face of the boy as he practices tying
His father's tie there in secret,

And the face of that father,
Still warm with the mystery of lather.
15 They are more fathers than sons themselves now.
Something is filling them, something

That is like the twilight sound
Of the crickets, immense,
Filling the woods at the foot of the slope
Behind their mortgaged houses.

THE TOURIST FROM SYRACUSE

One of those men who can be a car salesman or a tourist
from Syracuse or a hired assassin.

       —John D. MacDonald

You would not recognize me.
Mine is the face which blooms in
The dank mirrors of washrooms
As you grope for the light switch.

5 My eyes have the expression
Of the cold eyes of statues
Watching their pigeons return
From the feed you have scattered,

And I stand on my corner
10 With the same marble patience.
If I move at all, it is
At the same pace precisely

As the shade of the awning
Under which I stand waiting
15 And with whose blackness it seems
I am already blended.

I speak seldom, and always
In a murmur as quiet
As that of crowds which surround
20 The victims of accidents.

Shall I confess who I am?
My name is all names and none.
I am the used-car salesman,
The tourist from Syracuse,

25 The hired assassin, waiting.
I will stand here forever
Like one who has missed his bus—
Familiar, anonymous—

On my usual corner,
30 The corner at which you turn
To approach that place where now
You must not hope to arrive.

Sleepily, the muse to me: "Let us be friends.
Good friends, but only friends. You understand."
And yawned. And kissed, for the last time, my ear.
Who earlier, weeping at my touch, had whispered:
"I loved you once." And: "No, I don't love him,
Not after everything he did." Later,
Rebuttoning her nightgown with my help:
"Sorry, I just have no desire, it seems."
Sighing: "For you, I mean." Long silence. Then:
"You always were so serious." At which
I smiled, darkly. And that was how I came
To sleep beside, not with her; without dreams.

I call her up sometimes, long distance now.
And she still knows my voice, but I can hear,
Beyond the music of her phonograph,
The laughter of the young men with their keys.

I have the number written down somewhere.

This poem is not addressed to you.
You may come into it briefly,
But no one will find you here, no one.
You will have changed before the poem will.

5   Even while you sit there, unmovable,
You have begun to vanish. And it does not matter.
The poem will go on without you.
It has the spurious glamor of certain voids.

It is not sad, really, only empty.
10   Once perhaps it was sad, no one knows why.
It prefers to remember nothing.
Nostalgias were peeled from it long ago.

Your type of beauty has no place here.
Night is the sky over this poem.
15   It is too black for stars.
And do not look for any illumination.

You neither can nor should understand what it means.
Listen, it comes without guitar,
Neither in rags nor any purple fashion.
20   And there is nothing in it to comfort you.

Close your eyes, yawn. It will be over soon.
You will forget the poem, but not before
It has forgotten you. And it does not matter.
It has been most beautiful in its erasures.

25   O bleached mirrors! Oceans of the drowned!
Nor is one silence equal to another.
And it does not matter what you think.
This poem is not addressed to you.

He has come to report himself
A missing person.

The authorities
Hand him the forms.

5   He knows how they have waited
With the learned patience of barbers

In small shops, idle,
Stropping their razors.

But now that these spaces in his life
10   Stare up at him blankly,

Waiting to be filled in,
He does not know how to begin.

Afraid that he may not answer
To his description of himself,

15   He asks for a mirror.
They reassure him

That he can be nowhere
But wherever he finds himself

From moment to moment
20   Which, for the moment, is here.

And he might like to believe them.
But in the mirror

He sees what is missing.
It is himself

25 He sees there emerging
Slowly, as from the dark

Of a furnished room
Only by darkness,

One who receives no mail
30 And is known to the landlady only

For keeping himself to himself,
And for whom it will be years yet

Before he can trust to the light
This last disguise, himself.

MAXINE KUMIN

1925–

Born in Philadelphia and educated at Radcliffe, Maxine Kumin is the author of several books of poetry, essays, and novels, as well as more than twenty children's stories, three of which she wrote with Anne Sexton. Her poetry often focuses on suburban life and its ambivalent connection to the natural world. At the age of seventy-three, Kumin suffered a near fatal accident. She wrote about the experience and her recovery in a memoir, *Inside the Halo and Beyond*.

I write from a woman's perspective because I am a woman. It is as simple as that. I'm attracted to certain subjects because of my gender, and there are certain subjects I clearly can write about that perhaps a man can't.

MORNING SWIM

Into my empty head there come
a cotton beach, a dock wherefrom

I set out, oily and nude
through mist, in chilly solitude.

5   There was no line, no roof or floor
to tell the water from the air.

Night fog thick as terry cloth
closed me in its fuzzy growth.

I hung my bathrobe on two pegs.
10   I took the lake between my legs.

Invaded and invader, I
went overhand on that flat sky.

Fish twitched beneath me, quick and tame.
In their green zone they sang my name

15   and in the rhythm of the swim
I hummed a two-four-time slow hymn.

I hummed "Abide With Me." The beat
rose in the fine thrash of my feet,

rose in the bubbles I put out
20   slantwise, trailing through my mouth.

My bones drank water; water fell
through all my doors. I was the well

that fed the lake that met my sea
in which I sang "Abide With Me."

Afterward, the compromise.
Bodies resume their boundaries.

These legs, for instance, mine.
Your arms take you back in.

5   Spoons of our fingers, lips
admit their ownership.

The bedding yawns, a door
blows aimlessly ajar

and overhead, a plane
10   singsongs coming down.

Nothing is changed, except
there was a moment when

the wolf, the mongering wolf
who stands outside the self

lay lightly down, and slept.

Can it be
I am the only Jew residing in Danville, Kentucky,
looking for matzoh in the Safeway and the A & P?
The Sears Roebuck salesman wrapping my potato masher
5   advises me to accept Christ as my personal saviour
or else when I die I'll drop straight down to hell,
but the ladies who come knocking with their pamphlets
say as long as I believe in God that makes us
sisters in Christ. I thank them kindly.

10   In the county there are thirty-seven churches
and no butcher shop. This could be taken
as a matter of all form and no content.
On the other hand, form can be seen as
an extension of content, I have read that,
15   up here in the sealed-off wing where my three rooms
are threaded by outdoor steps to the downstairs world.
In the open risers walnut trees are growing.
Sparrows dipped in raspberry juice
come to my one windowsill. Cardinals
20   are blood spots before my eyes.
My bed is a narrow canoe with a fringy throw.
Whenever I type it takes to the open sea
and comes back wrong end to.
Every morning the pillows produce tapioca.
25   I gather it up for a future banquet.

I am leading a meatless life. I keep
my garbage in the refrigerator. Eggshells
potato peels and the rinds of cheeses nest
in the empty sockets of my daily grapefruit.
Every afternoon at five I am comforted
by the carillons of the Baptist church next door.
I let the rock of ages cleave for me on Monday.
Tuesday I am washed in the blood of the lamb.
Bringing in the sheaves on Wednesday keeps me busy.
Thursday's the day on Christ the solid rock I stand.
The Lord lifts me up to higher ground on Friday so that
Saturday I put my hands in the nail-scarred hands.
Nevertheless, I stay put on the Sabbath. I let
the whiskey bottle say something scurrilous.

Jesus, if you are in all thirty-seven churches,
are you not also here with me
making it alone in my back rooms like a flagpole sitter
slipping my peanut shells and prune pits into the Kelvinator?
Are you not here at nightfall
ticking in the box of the electric blanket?
Lamb, lamb, let me give you honey on your grapefruit
and toast for the birds to eat
out of your damaged hands.

When the barn catches fire
I am wearing the wrong negligee.
It hangs on me like a gunny sack.
I get the horses out, but they
wrench free, wheel, dash back
and three or four trips are required.
Much whinnying and rearing as well.
This happens whenever I travel.

At the next stopover, the children take off
their doctor and lawyer disguises
and turn back into little lambs.
They cower at windows from which flames
shoot like the tattered red cloth
of dimestore devil suits. They refuse
to jump into my waiting arms, although
I drilled them in this technique, years ago.

Finally they come to their senses and leap
but each time, the hoop holds my mother.
Her skin is as dry and papery
as a late onion. I take her
into my bed, an enormous baby
I do not especially want to keep.
Three nights of such disquiet
in and out of dreams as thin as acetate

25 until, last of all, it's you
    trapped in the blazing fortress.
    I hold the rope as you slide from danger.
    It's tricky in high winds and drifting snow.
    Your body swaying in space
30 grows heavier, older, stranger

    and me in the same gunny sack
    and the slamming sounds as the gutted building burns.
    Now the family's out, there's no holding back.
    I go in to get my turn.

Shall I say how it is in your clothes?
A month after your death I wear your blue jacket.
The dog at the center of my life recognizes
you've come to visit, he's ecstatic.
5   In the left pocket, a hole.
In the right, a parking ticket
delivered up last August on Bay State Road.
In my heart, a scatter like milkweed,
a flinging from the pods of the soul.
10   My skin presses your old outline.
It is hot and dry inside.

I think of the last day of your life,
old friend, how I would unwind it, paste
it together in a different collage,
15   back from the death car idling in the garage,
back up the stairs, your praying hands unlaced,
reassembling the bits of bread and tuna fish
into a ceremony of sandwich,
running the home movie backward to a space
20   we could be easy in, a kitchen place
with vodka and ice, our words like living meat.

Dear friend, you have excited crowds
with your example. They swell
like wine bags, straining at your seams.
25   I will be years gathering up our words,
fishing out letters, snapshots, stains,
leaning my ribs against this durable cloth
to put on the dumb blue blazer of your death.

ROBERT BLY

1926–

Robert Bly was born in Minnesota, where he still lives. After serving in the navy during World War II, he graduated from Harvard, attending at the same time as Donald Hall and Adrienne Rich, and later spent two years at the Iowa Writers' Workshop. Bly is also a translator, editor, and publisher. He is the founder of a journal series for poetry translation, first titled *The Fifties* and renamed with each new decade. In 1966, Bly cofounded American Writers Against the Vietnam War, and in 1969 he donated his prize money from the National Book Award to a draft resistance organization. He has published over thirty books of poetry and is also well known as the writer of *Iron John: A Book About Men,* a nonfiction work about masculinity in American culture.

When I first began writing poems about box turtles or the feet of wrens, I wanted to be pure: I wanted to have the description free of my Americanness or my sadness. I wanted their colors in the poem, not mine. But if colors don't come in from my psyche, there won't be any colors. There'll only be a negative.

Andrew Jackson

I want to be a white horse!
I want to be a white horse on the green mountains!
A horse that runs over wooden bridges and sleeps
In abandoned barns. . . .

Theodore Roosevelt

5 When I was President, I crushed snails with my bare teeth.
I slept in my underwear in the White House.
I ate the Cubans with a straw, and Lenin dreamt of *me* every night.
I wore down a forest of willow trees. I ground the snow,
And sold it.
10 The mountains of Texas shall heal our cornfields,
Overrun by the yellow race.
As for me, I want to be a stone! Yes!
I want to be a stone laid down thousands of years ago,
A stone with almost invisible cracks!
15 I want to be a stone that holds up the edge of the lake house,
A stone that suddenly gets up and runs around at night,
And lets the marriage bed fall; a stone that leaps into the water,
Carrying the robber down with him.

JOHN F. KENNEDY

I want to be a stream of water falling—
20 Water falling from high in the mountains, water
That dissolves everything,
And is never drunk, falling from ledge to ledge, from glass to glass.
I want the air around me to be invisible, resilient,
Able to flow past rocks.
25 I will carry the boulders with me to the valley.
Then ascending I will fall through space again:
Glittering in the sun, like the crystal in sideboards,
Goblets of the old life, before it was ruined by the Church.
And when I ascend the third time, I will fall forever,
Missing the earth entirely.

I start out for a walk at last after weeks at the desk.
Moon gone, plowing underfoot, no stars; not a trace of light!
Suppose a horse were galloping toward me in this open field?
Every day I did not spend in solitude was wasted.

1

Walking north toward the point, I come on a dead seal. From a few feet away, he looks like a brown log. The body is on its back, dead only a few hours. I stand and look at him. There's a quiver in the dead flesh: My God, he's still alive. And a shock goes through me, as if a wall of my room had fallen away.

His head is arched back, the small eyes closed; the whiskers sometimes rise and fall. He is dying. This is the oil. Here on its back is the oil that heats our houses so efficiently. Wind blows fine sand back toward the ocean. The flipper near me lies folded over the stomach, looking like an unfinished arm, lightly glazed with sand at the edges. The other flipper lies half underneath. And the seal's skin looks like an old overcoat, scratched here and there—by sharp mussel shells maybe.

I reach out and touch him. Suddenly he rears up, turns over. He gives three cries: Awaark! Awaark! Awaark!—like the cries from Christmas toys. He lunges toward me; I am terrified and leap back, though I know there can be no teeth in that jaw. He starts flopping toward the sea. But he falls over, on his face. He does not want to go back to the sea. He looks up at the sky, and he looks like an old lady who has lost her hair. He puts his chin back down on the sand, rearranges his flippers, and waits for me to go. I go.

2

The next day I go back to say good-bye. He's dead now. But he's not. He's a quarter mile farther up the shore. Today he is thinner, squatting on his stomach, head out. The ribs show more: each vertebra on the back under the coat is visible, shiny. He breathes in and out.

A wave comes in, touches his nose. He turns and looks at me—the eyes slanted; the crown of his head looks like a boy's leather jacket bending over some bicycle bars. He is taking a long time to die. The whiskers white as porcupine quills, the forehead slopes. . . . Good-bye, brother, die in the sound of the waves. Forgive us if we have killed you. Long live your race, your inner-tube race, so uncomfortable on land, so comfortable in the ocean. Be comfortable in death then, when the sand will be out of your nostrils, and you can swim in long loops through the pure death, ducking under as assassinations break above you. You don't want to be touched by me. I climb the cliff and go home the other way.

In rainy September, when leaves grow down into the dark,
I put my forehead down to the damp, seaweed-smelling sand.
The time has come. I have put off choosing for years,
Perhaps whole lives. The fern has no choice but to live;
5   For this crime it receives earth, water, and night.

We close the door. "I have no claim on you." Dusk
Comes. You say, "The love I had with you is enough."
We know we could live apart from one another.
The sheldrake floats apart from the flock.
10   The oak tree puts out leaves alone on the lonely hillside.

Men and women before us have accomplished this.
I would see you, and you me, once a year.
We would be two kernels, and not be planted.
We stay in the room, door closed, lights out.
I weep with you without shame and without honor.

In late September many voices
Tell you you will die.
That leaf says it. That coolness.
All of them are right.

5 Our many souls—what
Can they do about it?
Nothing. They're already
Part of the invisible.

Our souls have been
10 Longing to go home
Anyway. "It's late," they say.
"Lock the door, let's go."

The body doesn't agree. It says,
"We buried a little iron
15 Ball under that tree.
Let's go get it."

Think in ways you've never thought before.
If the phone rings, think of it as carrying a message
Larger than anything you've ever heard,
Vaster than a hundred lines of Yeats.

5 Think that someone may bring a bear to your door,
Maybe wounded and deranged; or think that a moose
Has risen out of the lake, and he's carrying on his antlers
A child of your own whom you've never seen.

When someone knocks on the door, think that he's about
10 To give you something large: tell you you're forgiven,
Or that it's not necessary to work all the time, or that it's
Been decided that if you lie down no one will die.

ROBERT CREELEY

1926–

Educated at Harvard, Robert Creeley dropped out shortly before earning his bachelor's degree. Twelve years later, although already established as a teacher, writer, and editor, he earned a master's degree from the University of New Mexico. Creeley lived abroad for many years, first as an ambulance driver in Burma and India and later with his family in France and Spain. As an instructor at Black Mountain College and the first editor of *The Black Mountain Review,* Creeley helped define the literary landscape of the 1950s. He names Ezra Pound, William Carlos Williams, and Charles Olson as his progenitors, and through his prolific publishing—more than a dozen volumes of poetry—and legendary teaching at the State University of New York at Buffalo, he has influenced a generation of American poets.

I think if it isn't fun, it isn't a poem.

THE INNOCENCE

Looking to the sea, it is a line
of unbroken mountains.

It is the sky.
It is the ground. There
5   we live, on it.

It is a mist
now tangent to another
quiet. Here the leaves
come, there
10   is the rock in evidence

or evidence.
What I come to do
is partial, partially kept.

As I sd to my
friend, because I am
always talking,—John, I

sd, which was not his
name, the darkness sur-
rounds us, what

can we do against
it, or else, shall we &
why not, buy a goddamn big car,

drive, he sd, for
christ's sake, look
out where yr going.

THE RAIN

All night the sound had
come back again,
and again falls
this quiet, persistent rain.

5   What am I to myself
that must be remembered,
insisted upon
so often? Is it

that never the ease,
10   even the hardness,
of rain falling
will have for me

something other than this,
something not so insistent—
15   am I to be locked in this
final uneasiness.

Love, if you love me,
lie next to me.
Be for me, like rain,
20   the getting out

of the tiredness, the fatuousness, the semi-
lust of intentional indifference.
Be wet
with a decent happiness.

Locate *I*
love you some-
where in

teeth and
5   eyes, bite
it but

take care not
to hurt, you
want so

10   much so
little. Words
say everything,

I
love you
15   again,

then what
is emptiness
for. To

fill, fill.
20   I heard words
and words full

of holes
aching. Speech
is a mouth.

ARROYO

Out the window,
across the ground there,
persons walk
in the hard sun—

5 Like years ago we'd watch
the children go to school
in the vacant building now
across the arroyo.

Same persons,
10 Mr. Gutierrez and,
presumably, his son,
Victor, back from the army—

Would wave to me
if I did to them,
15 call *que tal, hello,*
across the arroyo.

How sentimental,
heartfelt, this life becomes
when you try to think of it,
20 say it in simple words—

How far in time and space
the distance,
the simple division of a ditch,
between people.

This day after
Thanksgiving the edge
of winter
comes closer.

5   This grey, dulled
morning the sky
closes down on
the horizon to make

one wonder
10   if a life lives more
than just looking,
knowing nothing more.

Yet such a gentle
light, faded,
15   domestic,
impermanent—

one will not
go farther than home
to see this world
so quietly, greyly, shrunken.

SELF-PORTRAIT

He wants to be
a brutal old man,
an aggressive old man,
as dull, as brutal
5   as the emptiness around him,

He doesn't want compromise,
nor to be ever nice
to anyone. Just mean,
and final in his brutal,
10   his total, rejection of it all.

He tried the sweet,
the gentle, the "oh,
let's hold hands together"
and it was awful,
15   dull, brutally inconsequential.

Now he'll stand on
his own dwindling legs.
His arms, his skin,
shrink daily. And
he loves, but hates equally.

If happiness were
simple joy, bird,

beast or flower
were the so-called world

5   here everywhere
about us,

then love were as true
as air, as water—

as sky's light, ground's
10   solidness, rock's hardness,

for us, in us,
of us.

               ROBERT CREELEY

1

Dumbass clunk plane "American
Airlines" (well-named) waits at gate

for hour while friend in Nevada's
burned to ash. The rabbi

won't be back till Sunday.
Business lumbers on

in cheapshit world of
fake commerce, *buy and sell,*

what today, what
tomorrow. Friend's dead—

out of it, won't be back
to pay phoney dues. The best

conman in country's
gone and you're left in

plane's metal tube squeezed out
of people's pockets, pennies

it's made of, *big bucks,*
nickles, dimes all the same.

You won't understand it's forever—
one time, just *one time*

you get to play,
go for broke, *forever,* like

old-time musicians,
Thelonious, Bud Powell, Bird's

25   horn with the chewed-through reed,
Jamaica Plain in the 40s

—Izzy Ort's, The Savoy. Hi Hat's
now gas station. It goes fast.

Scramble it, make an omelet
30   out of it, for the hell of it. Eat

these sad pieces. Say it's
paper you wrote the world on

and guy's got gun to your head—
go on, he says, *eat it . . .*

35   You can't take it back.
It's gone. Max's dead.

2

What's memory's
agency—why so much
matter. Better remember

40   all one can forever—
never, *never* forget.
We met in Boston,

1947, he was out of jail
and just married, lived
45   in sort of hotel-like

room off Washington Street,
all the lights on,
a lot of them. I never

got to know her well,
50   Ina, but his daughter
Rachel I can think of

now, when she was 8,
stayed with us, Placitas, wanted bicycle,
big open-faced kid, loved

55   Max, her father, who,
in his own fragile way,
was good to her.

In and out
of time, first Boston,
60   New York later—then

he showed up in N.M.,
as I was leaving, 1956,
had the rent still paid

for three weeks on
65   "The Rose-Covered Cottage" in Ranchos
(*where sheep ambled o'er bridge*)

so we stayed,
worked the street, like they say,
lived on nothing.

70   Fast flashes—the women
who love him, Rena, Joyce,
Max, the *mensch*, makes

poverty almost fun,
hangs on edge, keeps traveling.
75   Israel—they catch him,

he told me, lifting
a bottle of scotch at the airport,
tch, tch, let him stay

(I now think) 'cause
80   he wants to.
Lives on kibbutz.

So back to New Mexico,
goyims' Israel sans the plan
save Max's ("Kansas City," "Terre Haute")

85   *New Buffalo* (friend told me
he yesterday saw that on bus placard
and thought, that's it! Max's place.)

People and people and people.
Buddy, Wuzza, Si
90   Perkoff, and Sascha,

Big John C., and Elaine,
the kids. Joel and Gil,
LeRoi, Cubby, back and back

to the curious end
95   where it bends away into
nowhere or Christmas he's

in the army, has come home,
and father, in old South Station,
turns him in as deserter, ashamed,

100 *ashamed* of his son. Or the man
Max then kid with his papers
met nightly at Summer Street

subway entrance and on Xmas
he gives him a dime for a tip . . .
105 No, old man, your son

was not wrong. "America"
just a vagueness, another place,
works for nothing, gets along . . .

3

In air
110 there's nowhere
enough not
here, nothing

left to speak
to but you'll
115 know as plane
begins its

descent, like
they say, it
was the place
120 where you were,

Santa Fe
(holy fire) with
mountains
of blood.

4

125 Can't leave, never could,
  without more, just
  one more

  for the road.
  Time to go makes
130 me stay—

  Max, *be happy*,
  be good, broken
  brother, *my man*, useless

  words
135 now
  forever.

FOR MAX FINSTEIN
DIED CIRCA 11:00 A.M. DRIVING TRUCK (HARVEY MUDD'S)
TO CALIFORNIA—NEAR LAS VEGAS—3/17/82

ALLEN GINSBERG

1926–1997

The son of a conventional lyric poet, Allen Ginsberg became a central figure in the beat movement. His life and writings were dedicated to defying convention and discovering beauty and meaning in places few are tempted to look—among drug addicts, the insane, and exiles of all kinds. His first book of poetry, *Howl and Other Poems,* was seized by San Francisco police and U.S. Customs officers as obscene and indecent. The resulting obscenity trial secured Ginsberg's fame and the success of his publisher, City Lights Books. Born to a secular Jewish family, Ginsberg studied with Vajradhatu Buddhist leader Chogyam Trungpa for twenty years. Spiritual yearning holds a central place in Ginsberg's poetry; this and his continuous resistance to authority have made Ginsberg a favorite of three generations of young people around the world.

Poetry is the record of individual insights into the secret soul of the individual and because all individuals are one in the eyes of their creator, into the soul of the world. The world has a soul.

FOR NAOMI GINSBERG, 1894–1956

Strange now to think of you, gone without corsets & eyes, while I walk on
the sunny pavement of Greenwich Village.
downtown Manhattan, clear winter noon, and I've been up all night, talking, talking, reading the Kaddish aloud, listening to Ray Charles blues
shout blind on the phonograph
the rhythm the rhythm—and your memory in my head three years after—
And read Adonais' last triumphant stanzas aloud—wept, realizing how
we suffer—
And how Death is that remedy all singers dream of, sing, remember, proph-
esy as in the Hebrew Anthem, or the Buddhist Book of Answers—and
my own imagination of a withered leaf—at dawn—

5   Dreaming back thru life, Your time—and mine accelerating toward
Apocalypse,
the final moment—the flower burning in the Day—and what comes after,
looking back on the mind itself that saw an American city
a flash away, and the great dream of Me or China, or you and a phantom
Russia, or a crumpled bed that never existed—
like a poem in the dark—escaped back to Oblivion—

10 No more to say, and nothing to weep for but the Beings in the Dream,
trapped in its disappearance,
sighing, screaming with it, buying and selling pieces of phantom, worshipping each other,
worshipping the God included in it all—longing or inevitability?—while it
lasts, a Vision—anything more?
It leaps about me, as I go out and walk the street, look back over my shoulder,
Seventh Avenue, the battlements of window office buildings shouldering
each other high, under a cloud, tall as the sky an instant—and the sky
above—an old blue place.

or down the Avenue to the south, to—as I walk toward the Lower East
     Side—where you walked 50 years ago, little girl—from Russia, eating
     the first poisonous tomatoes of America—frightened on the dock—

15   then struggling in the crowds of Orchard Street toward what?—toward
     Newark—

toward candy store, first home-made sodas of the century, hand-churned ice
     cream in backroom on musty brownfloor boards—

Toward education marriage nervous breakdown, operation, teaching school,
     and learning to be mad, in a dream—what is this life?

Toward the Key in the window—and the great Key lays its head of light on
     top of Manhattan, and over the floor, and lays down on the sidewalk—
     in a single vast beam, moving, as I walk down First toward the Yiddish
     Theater—and the place of poverty

you knew, and I know, but without caring now—Strange to have moved
     thru Paterson, and the West, and Europe and here again,

20   with the cries of Spaniards now in the doorstoops doors and dark boys on
     the street, fire escapes old as you

—Tho you're not old now, that's left here with me—

Myself, anyhow, maybe as old as the universe—and I guess that dies with
     us—enough to cancel all that comes—What came is gone forever every
     time—

That's good! That leaves it open for no regret—no fear radiators, lacklove,
     torture even toothache in the end—

Though while it comes it is a lion that eats the soul—and the lamb, the
     soul, in us, alas, offering itself in sacrifice to change's fierce hunger—
     hair and teeth—and the roar of bonepain, skull bare, break rib, rot-
     skin, braintricked Implacability.

25   Ai! ai! we do worse! We are in a fix! And you're out, Death let you out,
     Death had the Mercy, you're done with your century, done with God,
     done with the path thru it—Done with yourself at last—Pure—Back to
     the Babe dark before your Father, before us all—before the world—

There, rest. No more suffering for you. I know where you've gone, it's good.

No more flowers in the summer fields of New York, no joy now, no more fear of Louis,

and no more of his sweetness and glasses, his high school decades, debts, loves, frightened telephone calls, conception beds, relatives, hands—

No more of sister Elanor,—she gone before you—we kept it secret—you killed her—or she killed herself to bear with you—an arthritic heart—But Death's killed you both—No matter—

Nor your memory of your mother, 1915 tears in silent movies weeks and weeks—forgetting, agrieve watching Marie Dressler address humanity, Chaplin dance in youth,

or Boris Godunov, Chaliapin's at the Met, halling his voice of a weeping Czar—by standing room with Elanor & Max—watching also the Capitalists take seats in Orchestra, white furs, diamonds,

with the YPSL's hitch-hiking thru Pennsylvania, in black baggy gym skirts pants, photograph of 4 girls holding each other round the waste, and laughing eye, too coy, virginal solitude of 1920

all girls grown old, or dead, now, and that long hair in the grave—lucky to have husbands later—

You made it—I came too—Eugene my brother before (still grieving now and will gream on to his last stiff hand, as he goes thru his cancer—or kill—later perhaps—soon he will think—)

And it's the last moment I remember, which I see them all, thru myself, now—tho not you

I didn't foresee what you felt—what more hideous gape of bad mouth came first—to you—and were you prepared?

To go where? In that Dark—that—in that God? a radiance? A Lord in the Void? Like an eye in the black cloud in a dream? Adonoi at last, with you?

Beyond my remembrance! Incapable to guess! Not merely the yellow skull in the grave, or a box of worm dust, and a stained ribbon—Deaths-head with Halo? can you believe it?

Is it only the sun that shines once for the mind, only the flash of existence, than none ever was?

40 Nothing beyond what we have—what you had—that so pitiful—yet Triumph,

to have been here, and changed, like a tree, broken, or flower—fed to the ground—but mad, with its petals, colored, thinking Great Universe, shaken, cut in the head, leaf stript, hid in an egg crate hospital, cloth wrapped, sore—freaked in the moon brain, Naughtless.

No flower like that flower, which knew itself in the garden, and fought the knife—lost

Cut down by an idiot Snowman's icy—even in the Spring—strange ghost thought—some Death—Sharp icicle in his hand—crowned with old roses—a dog for his eyes—cock of a sweatshop—heart of electric irons.

All the accumulations of life, that wear us out—clocks, bodies, consciousness, shoes, breasts—begotten sons—your Communism—'Paranoia' into hospitals.

45 You once kicked Elanor in the leg, she died of heart failure later. You of stroke. Asleep? within a year, the two of you, sisters in death. Is Elanor happy?

Max grieves alive in an office on Lower Broadway, lone large mustache over midnight Accountings, not sure. His life passes—as he sees—and what does he doubt now? Still dream of making money, or that might have made money, hired nurse, had children, found even your Immortality, Naomi?

I'll see him soon. Now I've got to cut through—to talk to you—as I didn't when you had a mouth.

Forever. And we're bound to that, Forever—like Emily Dickinson's horses—headed to the End.

They know the way—These Steeds—run faster than we think—it's our own life they cross—and take with them.

1959

FOURTH FLOOR, DAWN, UP ALL NIGHT WRITING LETTERS

Pigeons shake their wings on the copper church roof
out my window across the street, a bird perched on the cross
surveys the city's blue-grey clouds. Larry Rivers
'll come at 10 AM and take my picture. I'm taking
5   your picture, pigeons. I'm writing you down, Dawn.
I'm immortalizing your exhaust, Avenue A bus.
O Thought, now you'll have to think the same thing forever!

6:48 A.M. JUNE 7, 1980

I'll settle for Immortality—
Not thru the body
    Not thru the eyes
        Star-spangled high mountains
5   waning moon over Aspen peaks
But thru words, thru the breath
    of long sentences
loves I have, heart beating
    still,
10 inspiration continuous, exhalation of
    cadenced affection
These immortal survive America,
      survive the fall of States
    Departure of my body,
15   mouth dumb dust
This verse broadcasts desire,
      accomplishment of Desire
Now and forever boys can read
      girls dream, old men cry
20 Old women sigh
    youth still come.

July 19, 1992
Aspen

HOMELESS COMPLEYNT

Pardon me buddy, I didn't mean to bug you
        but I came from Vietnam
where I killed a lot of Vietnamese gentlemen
        a few ladies too
5 and I couldn't stand the pain
         and got a habit out of fear
& I've gone through rehab and I'm clean
        but I got no place to sleep
          and I don't know what to do
10   with myself right now

I'm sorry buddy, I didn't mean to bug you
        but it's cold in the alley
          & my heart's sick alone
and I'm clean, but my life's a mess
15   Third Avenue
         and E. Houston Street
on the corner traffic island under a red light
wiping your windshield with a dirty rag

DECEMBER 24, 1996

General Mother Teresa
      Emperor Dalai Lama XIV
        Chief of Staff Thich Nhat Hanh
        Army Chaplain John Paul II
followed by the shades of Gandhi
      Sakharov, Sartre & his uncle
        Albert Schweitzer
went to the bombed out streets
talked to Moslem Bosnians in
      the burnt out grocery stores
parlayed with Croatian & Serbian Generals & Parliament
asked them to quit shooting & firing
      artillery from the mountainside
overlooking villages
      emptied of grandmothers—
So now there was quiet—a few fires
      smoldered in back alleys
a few corpses stank in wet fields
—But who owns these houses? The
      cinema theaters with broken doors?
Who owns that grocery store, that City Hall,
      that windowless school with broken
      rooftiles?
Who owns these little apartments, now
      all worshippers of Allah
pray in towns besieged 100 miles away
overcrowded in tenements & tents, with
      U.N. portosans at the crossroads?
Who owns these abandoned alleys &
      drugstores with shattered bottle shards over
      the sidewalk & inside the door?

      ALLEN GINSBERG

Who'll be the judge, attorney, file
          legal briefs,
bankruptcy papers, affidavits of ownership,
                deeds, old tax receipts?
Who'll council who lives where in the rubble,
          who'll sleep in what brokenwalled hut
in the full moonlight when spring clouds
          pass over the face
of the man in the moon at the end of May?

MAY 6, 1993, 3 A.M.

FRANK O'HARA

1926–1966

Shortly after high school, Frank O'Hara enlisted in the navy, serving in the South Pacific and Japan during World War II. When he returned, he attended Harvard, where he took a particular interest in music and art, and began to write poetry. O'Hara continued his interest in other art forms, working at the Museum of Modern Art in New York City and occasionally collaborating with painters to make "poem-paintings"; he maintained friendships with Jackson Pollock, Franz Kline, and Willem de Kooning. A prolific writer, O'Hara became one of the leading figures in what would later be called the New York school of poetry.

As for measure and other technical apparatus, that's just common sense: if you're going to buy a pair of pants you want them to be tight enough so everyone will want to go to bed with you. There's nothing metaphysical about it.

I am not a painter, I am a poet.
Why? I think I would rather be
a painter, but I am not. Well,

for instance, Mike Goldberg
5   is starting a painting. I drop in.
"Sit down and have a drink" he
says. I drink; we drink. I look
up. "You have SARDINES in it."
"Yes, it needed something there."
10 "Oh." I go and the days go by
and I drop in again. The painting
is going on, and I go, and the days
go by. I drop in. The painting is
finished. "Where's SARDINES?"
15 All that's left is just
letters, "It was too much," Mike says.

But me? One day I am thinking of
a color: orange. I write a line
about orange. Pretty soon it is a
20 whole page of words, not lines.
Then another page. There should be
so much more, not of orange, of
words, of how terrible orange is
and life. Days go by. It is even in
25 prose, I am a real poet. My poem
is finished and I haven't mentioned
orange yet. It's twelve poems, I call
it ORANGES. And one day in a gallery
I see Mike's painting, called SARDINES.

The Sun woke me this morning loud
and clear, saying "Hey! I've been
trying to wake you up for fifteen
minutes. Don't be so rude, you are
5   only the second poet I've ever chosen
to speak to personally
                         so why
aren't you more attentive? If I could
burn you through the window I would
10   to wake you up. I can't hang around
here all day."
                "Sorry, Sun, I stayed
up late last night talking to Hal."

"When I woke up Mayakovsky he was
15   a lot more prompt" the Sun said
petulantly. "Most people are up
already waiting to see if I'm going
to put in an appearance."
                           I tried
20   to apologize "I missed you yesterday."
"That's better" he said. "I didn't
know you'd come out." "You may be
wondering why I've come so close?"
"Yes" I said beginning to feel hot
25   wondering if maybe he wasn't burning me
anyway.
         "Frankly I wanted to tell you
I like your poetry. I see a lot
on my rounds and you're okay. You may
30   not be the greatest thing on earth, but
you're different. Now, I've heard some

say you're crazy, they being excessively
calm themselves to my mind, and other
crazy poets think that you're a boring
35   reactionary. Not me.
                        Just keep on
like I do and pay no attention. You'll
find that people always will complain
about the atmosphere, either too hot
40   or too cold too bright or too dark, days
too short or too long.
                        If you don't appear
at all one day they think you're lazy
or dead. Just keep right on, I like it.

45   And don't worry about your lineage
poetic or natural. The Sun shines on
the jungle, you know, on the tundra
the sea, the ghetto. Wherever you were
I knew it and saw you moving. I was waiting
50   for you to get to work.

                        And now that you
are making your own days, so to speak,
even if no one reads you but me
you won't be depressed. Not
55   everyone can look up, even at me. It
hurts their eyes."
                        "Oh Sun, I'm so grateful to you!"

"Thanks and remember I'm watching. It's
easier for me to speak to you out
here. I don't have to slide down
between buildings to get your ear.
I know you love Manhattan, but
you ought to look up more often.
                              And
always embrace things, people earth
sky stars, as I do, freely and with
the appropriate sense of space. That
is your inclination, known in the heavens
and you should follow it to hell, if
necessary, which I doubt.
                          Maybe we'll
speak again in Africa, of which I too
am specially fond. Go back to sleep now
Frank, and I may leave a tiny poem
in that brain of yours as my farewell."

"Sun, don't go!" I was awake
at last. "No, go I must, they're calling
me."
      "Who are they?"
                        Rising he said "Some
day you'll know. They're calling to you
too." Darkly he rose, and then I slept.

THE DAY LADY DIED

It is 12:20 in New York a Friday
three days after Bastille day, yes
it is 1959 and I go get a shoeshine
because I will get off the 4:19 in Easthampton
at 7:15 and then go straight to dinner
and I don't know the people who will feed me

I walk up the muggy street beginning to sun
and have a hamburger and a malted and buy
an ugly NEW WORLD WRITING to see what the poets
in Ghana are doing these days
                              I go on to the bank
and Miss Stillwagon (first name Linda I once heard)
doesn't even look up my balance for once in her life
and in the GOLDEN GRIFFIN I get a little Verlaine
for Patsy with drawings by Bonnard although I do
think of Hesiod, trans. Richmond Lattimore or
Brendan Behan's new play or *Le Balcon* or *Les Nègres*
of Genet, but I don't, I stick with Verlaine
after practically going to sleep with quandariness

and for Mike I just stroll into the PARK LANE
Liquor Store and ask for a bottle of Strega and
then I go back where I came from to 6th Avenue
and the tobacconist in the Ziegfeld Theatre and
casually ask for a carton of Gauloises and a carton
of Picayunes, and a NEW YORK POST with her face on it

and I am sweating a lot by now and thinking of
leaning on the john door in the 5 SPOT
while she whispered a song along the keyboard
to Mal Waldron and everyone and I stopped breathing

I belong here. I was born
here. The palms sift their fingers
and the men shove by in shirts,
shaving in underwear shorts.
5   They curse and scratch the wet hair
in their armpits, and spit. Whores
spread their delicate little germs
or, indifferently, don't, smiling.
The waves wash in, warm and salty,
10   leaving your eyebrows white and
the edge of your cheekbone. Your ear
aches. You are lonely. On the
underside of the satin leaf, hot
with shade, a scorpion sleeps. And
15   one Sunday I will be shot brushing
my teeth. I am a native of this island.

You do not always know what I am feeling.
Last night in the warm spring air while I was
blazing my tirade against someone who doesn't
interest

5   me, it was love for you that set me
afire,

        and isn't it odd? for in rooms full of
strangers my most tender feelings

                          writhe and

10 bear the fruit of screaming. Put out your hand,
isn't there

        an ashtray, suddenly, there? beside
the bed? And someone you love enters the room
and says wouldn't

15   you like the eggs a little
different today?

        And when they arrive they are
just plain scrambled eggs and the warm weather
is holding.

Don't call to me father
wherever you are I'm
still your little son
running through the dark

5   I couldn't do what you
say even if I could hear
your roses no longer grow
my heart's black as their

bed their dainty thorns
10   have become my face's
troublesome stubble you
must not think of flowers

And do not frighten my
blue eyes with hazel flecks
15   or thicken my lips when
I face my mirror don't ask

that I be other than your
strange son understanding
minor miracles not death
20   father I am alive! father

forgive the roses and me

INTERIOR (WITH JANE)

The eagerness of objects to
be what we are afraid to do

cannot help but move us   Is
this willingness to be a motive

5   in us what we reject?   The
really stupid things, I mean

a can of coffee, a 35¢ ear
ring, a handful of hair, what

do these things do to us?   We
10   come into the room, the windows

are empty, the sun is weak
and slippery on the ice   And a

sob comes, simply because it is
coldest of the things we know

When I was a child
I played by myself in a
corner of the schoolyard
all alone.

5   I hated dolls and I
hated games, animals were
not friendly and birds
flew away.

If anyone was looking
10   for me I hid behind a
tree and cried out "I am
an orphan."

And here I am, the
center of all beauty!
15   writing these poems!
Imagine!

JAMES WRIGHT

1927–1980

Born in Martins Ferry, Ohio, to parents who never finished high school, James Wright served in the army during World War II and then earned a bachelor's degree from Kenyon College. He attended the University of Vienna as a Fulbright scholar and went on to earn a Ph.D. from the University of Washington. Citing Edwin Arlington Robinson and Robert Frost as his models, Wright published his first book of poetry while he was still a graduate student. His subsequent translations of Georg Trakl influenced much of the work that followed. In the early 1960s, Wright developed friendships with Robert Bly, John Logan, and Anne Sexton, and he collaborated with Bly on four books, translating the poems of Trakl, Cesar Vallejo, and Pablo Neruda.

I think that an intelligent poetry is a poetry whose author has
given a great deal of slow and silent attention to the problems of
craft; that is, how to say something and say it in a musical way,
but I feel that ultimately any writer has to come to terms
with ethical and epistemological questions about
the meaning of life and of his life.

SAINT JUDAS

When I went out to kill myself, I caught
A pack of hoodlums beating up a man.
Running to spare his suffering, I forgot
My name, my number, how my day began,
5   How soldiers milled around the garden stone
And sang amusing songs; how all that day
Their javelins measured crowds; how I alone
Bargained the proper coins, and slipped away.

Banished from heaven, I found this victim beaten,
10   Stripped, kneed, and left to cry. Dropping my rope
Aside, I ran, ignored the uniforms:
Then I remembered bread my flesh had eaten,
The kiss that ate my flesh. Flayed without hope,
I held the man for nothing in my arms.

In the Shreve High football stadium,
I think of Polacks nursing long beers in Tiltonsville,
And gray faces of Negroes in the blast furnace at Benwood,
And the ruptured night watchman of Wheeling Steel,
5   Dreaming of heroes.

All the proud fathers are ashamed to go home.
Their women cluck like starved pullets,
Dying for love.

Therefore,
10   Their sons grow suicidally beautiful
At the beginning of October,
And gallop terribly against each other's bodies.

LYING IN A HAMMOCK AT WILLIAM DUFFY'S FARM
IN PINE ISLAND, MINNESOTA

Over my head, I see the bronze butterfly,
Asleep on the black trunk,
Blowing like a leaf in green shadow.
Down the ravine behind the empty house,
5   The cowbells follow one another
Into the distances of the afternoon.
To my right,
In a field of sunlight between two pines,
The droppings of last year's horses
10   Blaze up into golden stones.
I lean back, as the evening darkens and comes on.
A chicken hawk floats over, looking for home.
I have wasted my life.

The moon drops one or two feathers into the field.

The dark wheat listens.

Be still.

Now.

5   There they are, the moon's young, trying

Their wings.

Between trees, a slender woman lifts up the lovely shadow

Of her face, and now she steps into the air, now she is gone

Wholly, into the air.

10   I stand alone by an elder tree, I do not dare breathe

Or move.

I listen.

The wheat leans back toward its own darkness,

And I lean toward mine.

HAVING LOST MY SONS, I CONFRONT THE WRECKAGE OF THE MOON: CHRISTMAS, 1960

After dark
Near the South Dakota border,
The moon is out hunting, everywhere,
Delivering fire,
5   And walking down hallways
Of a diamond.

Behind a tree,
It lights on the ruins
Of a white city:
10   Frost, frost.

Where are they gone,
Who lived there?

Bundled away under wings
And dark faces.

15   I am sick
Of it, and I go on,
Living, alone, alone,
Past the charred silos, past the hidden graves
Of Chippewas and Norwegians.

20   This cold winter
Moon spills the inhuman fire
Of jewels
Into my hands.

Dead riches, dead hands, the moon
25   Darkens,
And I am lost in the beautiful white ruins
Of America.

I renounce the blindness of the magazines.
I want to lie down under a tree.
This is the only duty that is not death.
This is the everlasting happiness
Of small winds.
Suddenly,
A pheasant flutters, and I turn
Only to see him vanishing at the damp edge
Of the road.

DONALD HALL

1928–

Donald Hall published his first poem at the age of sixteen. He followed that early debut with more than a dozen books of poetry, several books for children, short stories, plays, and nonfiction works on subjects that range from baseball to sculpture. In 1972, he married a fellow poet and former student, Jane Kenyon. In 1975, Hall quit his academic post at the University of Michigan and moved with Kenyon to the New Hampshire farm his great-grandfather had settled. He has continued to write prolifically, winning numerous honors and awards.

I write anytime I can write, but my habit is to work early in the morning. Typically, I get up at about five and read the paper, have breakfast, drink some coffee, and then get to my desk at about six or six-thirty. I work on poetry first, because it's hardest.

MY SON MY EXECUTIONER

My son, my executioner,
　　I take you in my arms,
Quiet and small and just astir
　　And whom my body warms.

5　Sweet death, small son, our instrument
　　Of immortality,
Your cries and hungers document
　　Our bodily decay.

We twenty-five and twenty-two,
10　Who seemed to live forever,
Observe enduring life in you
　　And start to die together.

One midnight, after a day when lilies
lift themselves out of the ground while you watch them,
and you come into the house at dark
your fingers grubby with digging, your eyes
5   vague with the pleasure of digging,

let a wind raised from the South
climb through your bedroom window, lift you in its arms
—you have become as small as a seed—
and carry you out of the house, over the black garden,
10   spinning and fluttering,

and drop you in cracked ground.
The dirt will be cool, rough to your clasped skin
like a man you have never known.
You will die into the ground
15   in a dead sleep, surrendered to water.

You will wake suffering
a widening pain in your side, a breach
gapped in your tight ribs
where a green shoot struggles to lift itself upwards
20   through the tomb of your dead flesh

to the sun, to the air of your garden
where you will blossom
in the shape of your own self, thoughtless
with flowers, speaking
to bees, in the language of green and yellow, white and red.

DONALD HALL

High on a slope in New Guinea
the Grumman Hellcat
lodges among bright vines
as thick as arms. In nineteen-forty-three,
5   the clenched hand of a pilot
glided it here
where no one has ever been.

In the cockpit the helmeted
skeleton sits
10   upright, held
by dry sinews at neck
and shoulder, and by webbing
that straps the pelvic cross
to the cracked
15   leather of the seat, and the breastbone
to the canvas cover
of the parachute.

Or say that the shrapnel
missed me, I flew
20   back to the carrier, and every morning
take the train, my pale
hands on a black case, and sit
upright, held
by the firm webbing.

My whole life has led me here.

Daisies made out of resin,
hairnets and submarines,
sandwiches, diaries, green
garden chairs,
and a thousand boxes of cough drops.

Three hundred years ago I was hedging
and ditching in Devon.

I lacked freedom of worship,
and freedom to trade molasses
for rum, for slaves, for molasses.

"I will sail to Massachusetts
to build the Kingdom
of Heaven on Earth!"

The side of a hill
swung open.
It was Woolworth's!

I followed this vision to Boston.

DONALD HALL

MAPLE SYRUP

August, goldenrod blowing. We walk
into the graveyard, to find
my grandfather's grave. Ten years ago
I came here last, bringing
     marigolds from the round garden
outside the kitchen.
I didn't know you then.

               We walk
among carved names that go with photographs
     on top of the piano at the farm:
Keneston, Wells, Fowler, Batchelder, Buck.
We pause at the new grave
of Grace Fenton, my grandfather's
sister. Last summer
     we called on her at the nursing home,
eighty-seven, and nodding
in a blue housedress. We cannot find
my grandfather's grave.

               Back at the house
     where no one lives, we potter
and explore the back chamber
where everything comes to rest: spinning wheels,
pretty boxes, quilts,
bottles, books, albums of postcards.
     Then with a flashlight we descend
firm steps to the root cellar—black,
cobwebby, huge,
with dirt floors and fieldstone walls,
and above the walls, holding the hewn
     sills of the house, enormous
granite foundation stones.
Past the empty bins

for squash, apples, carrots, and potatoes,
we discover the shelves for canning, a few
35   pale pints
of tomato left, and—what
is this?—syrup, maple syrup
in a quart jar, syrup
my grandfather made twenty-five
40   years ago
for the last time.
                              I remember
coming to the farm in March
in sugaring time, as a small boy.
45   He carried the pails of sap, sixteen-quart
buckets, dangling from each end
of a wooden yoke
that lay across his shoulders, and emptied them
into a vat in the saphouse
50   where fire burned day and night
for a week.
                              Now the saphouse
tilts, nearly to the ground,
like someone exhausted
55   to the point of death, and next winter
when snow piles three feet thick
on the roofs of the cold farm,
the saphouse will shudder and slide
with the snow to the ground.
60   Today
we take my grandfather's last
quart of syrup
upstairs, holding it gingerly,
and we wash off twenty-five years

65   of dirt, and we pull
    and pry the lid up, cutting the stiff,
    dried rubber gasket, and dip our fingers
    in, you and I both, and taste
    the sweetness, you for the first time,
70   the sweetness preserved, of a dead man
    in the kitchen he left
    when his body slid
    like anyone's into the ground.

1

Kicking the leaves, October, as we walk home together
from the game, in Ann Arbor,
on a day the color of soot, rain in the air;
I kick at the leaves of maples,
reds of seventy different shades, yellow
like old paper; and poplar leaves, fragile and pale;
and elm leaves, flags of a doomed race.
I kick at the leaves, making a sound I remember
as the leaves swirl upward from my boot,
and flutter; and I remember
Octobers walking to school in Connecticut,
wearing corduroy knickers that swished
with a sound like leaves; and a Sunday buying
a cup of cider at a roadside stand
on a dirt road in New Hampshire; and kicking the leaves,
autumn 1955 in Massachusetts, knowing
my father would die when the leaves were gone.

2

Each fall in New Hampshire, on the farm
where my mother grew up, a girl in the country,
my grandfather and grandmother
finished the autumn work, taking the last vegetables in
from the cold fields, canning, storing roots and apples
in the cellar under the kitchen. Then my grandfather
raked leaves against the house

DONALD HALL

25 as the final chore of autumn.
One November I drove up from college to see them.
We pulled big rakes, as we did when we hayed in summer,
pulling the leaves against the granite foundations
around the house, on every side of the house,
30 and then, to keep them in place, we cut spruce boughs
and laid them across the leaves,
green on red, until the house
was tucked up, ready for snow
that would freeze the leaves in tight, like a stiff skirt.
35 Then we puffed through the shed door,
taking off boots and overcoats, slapping our hands,
and sat in the kitchen, rocking, and drank
black coffee my grandmother made,
three of us sitting together, silent, in gray November.

3

40 One Saturday when I was little, before the war,
my father came home at noon from his half day at the office
and wore his Bates sweater, black on red,
with the crossed hockey sticks on it, and raked beside me
in the back yard, and tumbled in the leaves with me,
45 laughing, and carried me, laughing, my hair full of leaves,
to the kitchen window
where my mother could see us, and smile, and motion
to set me down, afraid I would fall and be hurt.

Kicking the leaves today, as we walk home together

50   from the game, among crowds of people

with their bright pennants, as many and bright as leaves,

my daughter's hair is the red-yellow color

of birch leaves, and she is tall like a birch,

growing up, fifteen, growing older; and my son

55   flamboyant as maple, twenty,

visits from college, and walks ahead of us, his step

springing, impatient to travel

the woods of the earth. Now I watch them

from a pile of leaves beside this clapboard house

60   in Ann Arbor, across from the school

where they learned to read,

as their shapes grow small with distance, waving,

and I know that I

diminish, not them, as I go first

65   into the leaves, taking

the way they will follow, Octobers and years from now.

5

This year the poems came back, when the leaves fell.
Kicking the leaves, I heard the leaves tell stories,
remembering, and therefore looking ahead, and building
the house of dying. I looked up into the maples
and found them, the vowels of bright desire.
I thought they had gone forever
while the bird sang *I love you, I love you*
and shook its black head
from side to side, and its red eye with no lid,
through years of winter, cold
as the taste of chickenwire, the music of cinderblock.

6

Kicking the leaves, I uncover the lids of graves.
My grandfather died at seventy-seven, in March
when the sap was running; and I remember my father
twenty years ago,
coughing himself to death at fifty-two in the house
in the suburbs. Oh, how we flung
leaves in the air! How they tumbled and fluttered around us,
like slowly cascading water, when we walked together
in Hamden, before the war, when Johnson's Pond
had not surrendered to houses, the two of us
hand in hand, and in the wet air the smell of leaves
burning;
and in six years I will be fifty-two.

7

Now I fall, now I leap and fall
to feel the leaves crush under my body, to feel my body
buoyant in the ocean of leaves, the night of them,
night heaving with death and leaves, rocking like the ocean.
95   Oh, this delicious falling into the arms of leaves,
into the soft laps of leaves!
Face down, I swim into the leaves, feathery,
breathing the acrid odor of maple, swooping
in long glides to the bottom of October—
100   where the farm lies curled against winter, and soup steams
its breath of onion and carrot
onto damp curtains and windows; and past the windows
I see the tall bare maple trunks and branches, the oak
with its few brown weathery remnant leaves,
105   and the spruce trees, holding their green.
Now I leap and fall, exultant, recovering
from death, on account of death, in accord with the dead,
the smell and taste of leaves again,
and the pleasure, the only long pleasure, of taking a place
in the story of leaves.

DONALD HALL

ANNE SEXTON

1928–1974

Perhaps as well known for her psychological problems and colorful persona as her poetry, Anne Sexton has become a popular feminist icon. She suffered a mental breakdown after the birth of her first child and spent the rest of her life in and out of institutions. Like Robert Lowell and Sylvia Plath, Sexton was first described as a confessional poet, but her later poetry shows a broad range of interests, including a fascination with other cultures. She experimented with both the form and the performance of poetry, using for a time a rock band to accompany her readings.

My poetry is very personal. I don't think I write public poems.
I write very personal poems but I hope that they will become
the central theme to someone else's private life.

HER KIND

I have gone out, a possessed witch,
haunting the black air, braver at night;
dreaming evil, I have done my hitch
over the plain houses, light by light:
5   lonely thing, twelve-fingered, out of mind.
A woman like that is not a woman, quite.
I have been her kind.

I have found the warm caves in the woods,
filled them with skillets, carvings, shelves,
10   closets, silks, innumerable goods;
fixed the suppers for the worms and the elves:
whining, rearranging the disaligned.
A woman like that is misunderstood.
I have been her kind.

15   I have ridden in your cart, driver,
waved my nude arms at villages going by,
learning the last bright routes, survivor
where your flames still bite my thigh
and my ribs crack where your wheels wind.
20   A woman like that is not ashamed to die.
I have been her kind.

**FOR MY FRIEND, RUTH, WHO URGES ME TO MAKE AN
APPOINTMENT FOR THE SACRAMENT OF CONFESSION**

Concerning your letter in which you ask
me to call a priest and in which you ask
me to wear The Cross that you enclose;
your own cross,
5   your dog-bitten cross,
no larger than a thumb,
small and wooden, no thorns, this rose—

I pray to its shadow,
that gray place
10   where it lies on your letter . . . deep, deep.
I detest my sins and I try to believe
in The Cross. I touch its tender hips, its dark jawed face,
its solid neck, its brown sleep.

True. There is
15   a beautiful Jesus.
He is frozen to his bones like a chunk of beef.
How desperately he wanted to pull his arms in!
How desperately I touch his vertical and horizontal axes!
But I can't. Need is not quite belief.

20   All morning long
I have worn
your cross, hung with package string around my throat.
It tapped me lightly as a child's heart might,
tapping secondhand, softly waiting to be born.
25   Ruth, I cherish the letter you wrote.

My friend, my friend, I was born
doing reference work in sin, and born
confessing it. This is what poems are:
with mercy
30   for the greedy,
they are the tongue's wrangle,
the world's pottage, the rat's star.

Some women marry houses.
It's another kind of skin; it has a heart,
a mouth, a liver and bowel movements.
The walls are permanent and pink.
See how she sits on her knees all day,
faithfully washing herself down.
Men enter by force, drawn back like Jonah
into their fleshy mothers.
A woman *is* her mother.
That's the main thing.

Just once I knew what life was for.
In Boston, quite suddenly, I understood;
walked there along the Charles River,
watched the lights copying themselves,
5 all neoned and strobe-hearted, opening
their mouths as wide as opera singers;
counted the stars, my little campaigners,
my scar daisies, and knew that I walked my love
on the night green side of it and cried
10 my heart to the eastbound cars and cried
my heart to the westbound cars and took
my truth across a small humped bridge
and hurried my truth, the charm of it, home
and hoarded these constants into morning
only to find them gone.

So it has come to this—
insomnia at 3:15 A.M.,
the clock tolling its engine

like a frog following
a sundial yet having an electric
seizure at the quarter hour.

The business of words keeps me awake.
I am drinking cocoa,
that warm brown mama.

I would like a simple life
yet all night I am laying
poems away in a long box.

It is my immortality box,
my lay-away plan,
my coffin.

All night dark wings
flopping in my heart.
Each an ambition bird.

The bird wants to be dropped
from a high place like Tallahatchie Bridge.

He wants to light a kitchen match
and immolate himself.

He wants to fly into the hand of Michelangelo
and come out painted on a ceiling.

He wants to pierce the hornet's nest
and come out with a long godhead.

He wants to take bread and wine
and bring forth a man happily floating in the Caribbean.

He wants to be pressed out like a key
30   so he can unlock the Magi.

He wants to take leave among strangers
passing out bits of his heart like hors d'oeuvres.

He wants to die changing his clothes
and bolt for the sun like a diamond.

35   He wants, I want.
Dear God, wouldn't it be
good enough to just drink cocoa?

I must get a new bird
and a new immortality box.
There is folly enough inside this one.

ADRIENNE RICH

1929–

Adrienne Rich is known for her writing in feminist and political theory as well as her poetry. Her early poems show an interest in formalism and a tendency toward restrained emotion, but her later work is often experimental in form and emotionally charged. Starting in the late 1950s, Rich added the date of composition to each poem as an argument against the view that poetry exists separately from a poet's life. During the 1960s and 1970s, her poetry reflected her growing interests in feminism, women's experience, and politics.

*Through its very being, poetry expresses messages beyond
the words it is contained in; it speaks of our desire;
it reminds us of what we lack, of our need, and of our
hungers. It keeps us dissatisfied. In that sense,
it can be very, very subversive.*

She had thought the studio would keep itself;
no dust upon the furniture of love.
Half heresy, to wish the taps less vocal,
the panes relieved of grime. A plate of pears,
5   a piano with a Persian shawl, a cat
stalking the picturesque amusing mouse
had risen at his urging.
Not that at five each separate stair would writhe
under the milkman's tramp; that morning light
10   so coldly would delineate the scraps
of last night's cheese and three sepulchral bottles;
that on the kitchen shelf among the saucers
a pair of beetle-eyes would fix her own—
envoy from some village in the moldings . . .
15   Meanwhile, he, with a yawn,
sounded a dozen notes upon the keyboard,
declared it out of tune, shrugged at the mirror,
rubbed at his beard, went out for cigarettes;
while she, jeered by the minor demons,
20   pulled back the sheets and made the bed and found
a towel to dust the table-top,
and let the coffee-pot boil over on the stove.
By evening she was back in love again,
though not so wholly but throughout the night
25   she woke sometimes to feel the daylight coming
like a relentless milkman up the stairs.

When the colossus of the will's dominion
Wavers and shrinks upon a dying eye,
Enormous shadows sit like birds of prey,
Waiting to fall where blistered marbles lie.

5   But in its open pools the place already
Lay ruined, before the old king left it free.
Shattered in waters of each marble basin
He might have seen it as today we see.

Dying in discontent, he must have known
10   How, once mere consciousness had turned its back,
The frescoes of his appetite would crumble,
The fountains of his longing yawn and crack.

And all his genius would become a riddle,
His perfect colonnades at last attain
15   The incompleteness of a natural thing;
His impulse turn to mystery again.

Who sleeps, and dreams, and wakes, and sleeps again
May dream again; so in the end we come
Back to the cherished and consuming scene
20   As if for once the stones will not be dumb.

We come like dreamers searching for an answer,
Passionately in need to reconstruct
The columned roofs under the blazing sky,
The courts so open, so forever locked.

25   And some of us, as dreamers, excavate
Under the blanching light of sleep's high noon,
The artifacts of thought, the site of love,
Whose Hadrian has given the slip, and gone.

ADRIENNE RICH

9/21/68

Violently asleep in the old house.
A clock stays awake all night ticking.

Turning, turning their bruised leaves
the trees stay awake all night in the wood.

5   Talk to me with your body through my dreams.
Tell me what we are going through.

The walls of the room are muttering,
old trees, old Utopians, arguing with the wind.

To float like a dead man in a sea of dreams
10   and half those dreams being dreamed by someone else.

Fifteen years of sleepwalking with you,
wading against the tide, and with the tide.

First having read the book of myths,
and loaded the camera,
and checked the edge of the knife-blade,
I put on
5   the body-armor of black rubber
the absurd flippers
the grave and awkward mask.
I am having to do this
not like Cousteau with his
10 assiduous team
aboard the sun-flooded schooner
but here alone.

There is a ladder.
The ladder is always there
15 hanging innocently
close to the side of the schooner.
We know what it is for,
we who have used it.
Otherwise
20 it's a piece of maritime floss
some sundry equipment.

I go down.
Rung after rung and still
the oxygen immerses me

25 the blue light
the clear atoms
of our human air.
I go down.
My flippers cripple me,

30 I crawl like an insect down the ladder
and there is no one
to tell me when the ocean
will begin.

First the air is blue and then

35 it is bluer and then green and then
black I am blacking out and yet
my mask is powerful
it pumps my blood with power
the sea is another story

40 the sea is not a question of power
I have to learn alone
to turn my body without force
in the deep element.

And now: it is easy to forget

45 what I came for
among so many who have always
lived here
swaying their crenellated fans
between the reefs

50 and besides
you breathe differently down here.

I came to explore the wreck.
The words are purposes.
The words are maps.
I came to see the damage that was done
and the treasures that prevail.
I stroke the beam of my lamp
slowly along the flank
of something more permanent
than fish or weed

the thing I came for:
the wreck and not the story of the wreck
the thing itself and not the myth
the drowned face always staring
toward the sun
the evidence of damage
worn by salt and sway into this threadbare beauty
the ribs of the disaster
curving their assertion
among the tentative haunters.

This is the place.
And I am here, the mermaid whose dark hair
streams black, the merman in his armored body
We circle silently
about the wreck
we dive into the hold.
I am she: I am he

ADRIENNE RICH

whose drowned face sleeps with open eyes
whose breasts still bear the stress
80   whose silver, copper, vermeil cargo lies
obscurely inside barrels
half-wedged and left to rot
we are the half-destroyed instruments
that once held to a course
85   the water-eaten log
the fouled compass

We are, I am, you are
by cowardice or courage
the one who find our way
90   back to this scene
carrying a knife, a camera
a book of myths
in which
our names do not appear.

1972

2

I wake up in your bed. I know I have been dreaming.
Much earlier, the alarm broke us from each other,
you've been at your desk for hours. I know what I dreamed:
our friend the poet comes into my room

5   where I've been writing for days,
drafts, carbons, poems are scattered everywhere,
and I want to show her one poem
which is the poem of my life. But I hesitate,
and wake. You've kissed my hair

10   to wake me. *I dreamed you were a poem,*
I say, *a poem I wanted to show someone . . .*
and I laugh and fall dreaming again
of the desire to show you to everyone I love,
to move openly together

15   in the pull of gravity, which is not simple,
which carries the feathered grass a long way down the upbreathing air.

ADRIENNE RICH

You: a woman too old
for passive contemplation
caught staring out a window
at bird-of-paradise spikes
5   jewelled with rain, across an alley
It's winter in this land
of roses, roses   sometimes
the fog lies thicker around you than your past
sometimes the Pacific radiance
10   scours the air to lapis
In this new world you feel
backward along the hem of your whole life
questioning every breadth
Nights you can watch the moon shed skin after skin
15   over and over, always a shape
of imbalance except
at birth and in the full
You, still trying to learn
how to live, what must be done
20   though in death you will be complete
whatever you do
But death is not the answer.

On these flat green leaves
light skates like a golden blade
25   high in the dull-green pine
sit two mushroom-colored doves
afterglow overflows
across the bungalow roof
between the signs for the three-way stop
30   over everything that is:
the cotton pants stirring on the line, the

empty Coke can by the fence
onto the still unflowering
mysterious acacia
35   and a sudden chill takes the air

Backward you dream to a porch
you stood on a year ago
snow flying quick as thought
sticking to your shoulder   gone
40   Blue shadows, ridged and fading
on a snow-swept road
the shortest day of the year
Backward you dream to glare ice
and ice-wet pussywillows
45   to Riverside Drive, the wind
cut loose from Hudson's Bay
driving tatters into your face
And back you come at last to that room
without a view, where webs of frost
50   blinded the panes at noon
where already you had begun
to make the visible world your conscience
asking things: *What can you tell me?*
what am I doing?   what must I do?

1985

GARY SNYDER

1930–

A pioneer in the study of Buddhism and Asian poetry, Gary Snyder spent twelve years in Japan, including three years in a Zen monastery. His poetry helped to inspire the environmental movement of the 1970s. Though Snyder was friends with Allen Ginsberg and Jack Kerouac (and the hero of Kerouac's novel *The Dharma Bums*), his poetry is closer in form to the Black Mountain school and closer in sympathy to the first-person political and personal poetry of Emily Dickinson and Edwin Arlington Robinson.

Poets, as few others, must live close to the world that primitive men are in: the world, in its nakedness, which is fundamental for all of us—birth, love, death; the sheer fact of being alive.

We finished clearing the last
Section of trail by noon,
High on the ridge-side
Two thousand feet above the creek
5   Reached the pass, went on
Beyond the white pine groves,
Granite shoulders, to a small
Green meadow watered by the snow,
Edged with Aspen—sun
10 Straight high and blazing
But the air was cool.
Ate a cold fried trout in the
Trembling shadows. I spied
A glitter, and found a flake
15 Black volcanic glass—obsidian—
By a flower. Hands and knees
Pushing the Bear grass, thousands
Of arrowhead leavings over a
Hundred yards. Not one good
20 Head, just razor flakes
On a hill snowed all but summer,
A land of fat summer deer,
They came to camp. On their
Own trails. I followed my own
25 Trail here. Picked up the cold-drill,
Pick, singlejack, and sack
Of dynamite.
Ten thousand years.

Goofing again
I shifted weight the wrong way
flipping the plank end-over
dumping me down in the bilge
5 & splatting a gallon can
of thick sticky dark red
italian deck paint
over the fresh white bulkhead.
such a trifling move
10 & such spectacular results.
now I have to paint the wall again
& salvage only from it all a poem.

Lay down these words
Before your mind like rocks.
    placed solid, by hands
In choice of place, set
5 Before the body of the mind
    in space and time:
Solidity of bark, leaf, or wall
    riprap of things:
Cobble of milky way,
10   straying planets,
These poems, people,
    lost ponies with
Dragging saddles
    and rocky sure-foot trails.
15 The worlds like an endless
    four-dimensional
Game of *Go*.
    ants and pebbles
In the thin loam, each rock a word
20   a creek-washed stone
Granite: ingrained
    with torment of fire and weight
Crystal and sediment linked hot
    all change, in thoughts,
As well as things.

sun breaks over the eucalyptus
grove below the wet pasture,
water's about hot,
I sit in the open window
5   & roll a smoke.

distant dogs bark, a pair of
cawing crows; the twang
of a pygmy nuthatch high in a pine—
from behind the cypress windrow
10   the mare moves up, grazing.

a soft continuous roar
comes out of the far valley
of the six-lane highway—thousands
and thousands of cars
driving men to work.

One afternoon the last week in April
Showing Kai how to throw a hatchet
One-half turn and it sticks in a stump.
He recalls the hatchet-head
5   Without a handle, in the shop
And go gets it, and wants it for his own.
A broken-off axe handle behind the door
Is long enough for a hatchet,
We cut it to length and take it
10   With the hatchet head
And working hatchet, to the wood block.
There I begin to shape the old handle
With the hatchet, and the phrase
First learned from Ezra Pound
15   Rings in my ears!
"When making an axe handle
      the pattern is not far off."
And I say this to Kai
"Look: We'll shape the handle
20   By checking the handle
Of the axe we cut with—"
And he sees. And I hear it again:
It's in Lu Ji's *Wên Fu*, fourth century
A.D. "Essay on Literature"—in the
25   Preface: "In making the handle
Of an axe
By cutting wood with an axe
The model is indeed near at hand."
My teacher Shih-hsiang Chen

30 Translated that and taught it years ago
And I see: Pound was an axe,
Chen was an axe, I am an axe
And my son a handle, soon
To be shaping again, model
35 And tool, craft of culture,
How we go on.

As for poets
The Earth Poets
Who write small poems,
Need help from no man.

5   The Air Poets
Play out the swiftest gales
And sometimes loll in the eddies.
Poem after poem,
Curling back on the same thrust.

10   At fifty below
Fuel oil won't flow
And propane stays in the tank.
Fire Poets
Burn at absolute zero
15   Fossil love pumped back up.

The first
Water Poet
Stayed down six years.
He was covered with seaweed.
20   The life in his poem
Left millions of tiny
Different tracks
Criss-crossing through the mud.

With the Sun and Moon
In his belly,
The Space Poet
Sleeps.
No end to the sky—
But his poems,
Like wild geese,
Fly off the edge.

A Mind Poet
Stays in the house.
The house is empty
And it has no walls.

The poem
Is seen from all sides,
Everywhere,
At once.

GARY SNYDER

I went into the Maverick Bar
In Farmington, New Mexico.
And drank double shots of bourbon
        backed with beer.
5 My long hair was tucked up under a cap
I'd left the earring in the car.

Two cowboys did horseplay
        by the pool tables,
A waitress asked us
10   where are you from?
a country-and-western band began to play
"We don't smoke Marijuana in Muskokie"
And with the next song,
        a couple began to dance.

15 They held each other like in High School dances
        in the fifties;
I recalled when I worked in the woods
        and the bars of Madras, Oregon.
That short-haired joy and roughness—
20   America—your stupidity.
I could almost love you again.

We left—onto the freeway shoulders—
        under the tough old stars—
In the shadow of bluffs
25   I came back to myself,
To the real work, to
        "What is to be done."

SYLVIA PLATH

1932–1963

An unrelenting fascination with the circumstances of Sylvia Plath's life—a stormy marriage to poet Ted Hughes, incarceration in an upscale mental hospital, difficulties with motherhood, and suicide at the age of thirty—has threatened to obscure her contribution as a poet: a mastery of craft demonstrating a remarkable balance between subject, image, and form. Born in a middle-class suburb of Boston, Plath began writing and publishing at a young age, graduating from Smith College and winning a Fulbright scholarship to Cambridge. Her internship at *Mademoiselle* magazine and her subsequent mental breakdown became the basis for her popular novel, *The Bell Jar*. Like the poetry of Anne Sexton and Robert Lowell, Plath's poems are confessional and confrontational in nature. In 1982, she was posthumously awarded the Pulitzer Prize for her *Collected Poems*.

I am a victim of introspection. If I have not the power to put myself in the place of other people, but must be continually burrowing inward, I shall never be the magnanimous creative person I wish to be.

THE COLOSSUS

I shall never get you put together entirely,
Pieced, glued, and properly jointed.
Mule-bray, pig-grunt and bawdy cackles
Proceed from your great lips.
5   It's worse than a barnyard.

Perhaps you consider yourself an oracle,
Mouthpiece of the dead, or of some god or other.
Thirty years now I have labored
To dredge the silt from your throat.
10 I am none the wiser.

Scaling little ladders with gluepots and pails of Lysol
I crawl like an ant in mourning
Over the weedy acres of your brow
To mend the immense skull-plates and clear
15 The bald, white tumuli of your eyes.

A blue sky out of the Oresteia
Arches above us. O father, all by yourself
You are pithy and historical as the Roman Forum.
I open my lunch on a hill of black cypress.
20 Your fluted bones and acanthine hair are littered

In their old anarchy to the horizon-line.
It would take more than a lightning-stroke
To create such a ruin.
Nights, I squat in the cornucopia
25 Of your left ear, out of the wind,

Counting the red stars and those of plum-color.
The sun rises under the pillar of your tongue.
My hours are married to shadow.
No longer do I listen for the scrape of a keel
On the blank stones of the landing.

I am silver and exact. I have no preconceptions.
Whatever I see I swallow immediately
Just as it is, unmisted by love or dislike.
I am not cruel, only truthful—
5   The eye of a little god, four-cornered.
Most of the time I meditate on the opposite wall.
It is pink, with speckles. I have looked at it so long
I think it is a part of my heart. But it flickers.
Faces and darkness separate us over and over.

10   Now I am a lake. A woman bends over me,
Searching my reaches for what she really is.
Then she turns to those liars, the candles or the moon.
I see her back, and reflect it faithfully.
She rewards me with tears and an agitation of hands.
15   I am important to her. She comes and goes.
Each morning it is her face that replaces the darkness.
In me she has drowned a young girl, and in me an old woman
Rises toward her day after day, like a terrible fish.

SYLVIA PLATH

I have done it again.
One year in every ten
I manage it——

A sort of walking miracle, my skin
5   Bright as a Nazi lampshade,
My right foot

A paperweight,
My face a featureless, fine
Jew linen.

10   Peel off the napkin
O my enemy.
Do I terrify?——

The nose, the eye pits, the full set of teeth?
The sour breath
15   Will vanish in a day.

Soon, soon the flesh
The grave cave ate will be
At home on me

And I a smiling woman.
20   I am only thirty.
And like the cat I have nine times to die.

This is Number Three.
What a trash
To annihilate each decade.

What a million filaments.
The peanut-crunching crowd
Shoves in to see

Them unwrap me hand and foot——
The big strip tease.
Gentlemen, ladies

These are my hands
My knees.
I may be skin and bone,

Nevertheless, I am the same, identical woman.
The first time it happened I was ten.
It was an accident.

The second time I meant
To last it out and not come back at all.
I rocked shut

As a seashell.
They had to call and call
And pick the worms off me like sticky pearls.

Dying
Is an art, like everything else.
I do it exceptionally well.

I do it so it feels like hell.
I do it so it feels real.
I guess you could say I've a call.

SYLVIA PLATH

It's easy enough to do it in a cell.
It's easy enough to do it and stay put.
It's the theatrical

Comeback in broad day
To the same place, the same face, the same brute
Amused shout:

"A miracle!"
That knocks me out.
There is a charge

For the eyeing of my scars, there is a charge
For the hearing of my heart——
It really goes.

And there is a charge, a very large charge
For a word or a touch
Or a bit of blood

Or a piece of my hair or my clothes.
So, so, Herr Doktor.
So, Herr Enemy.

I am your opus,
I am your valuable,
The pure gold baby

That melts to a shriek.
I turn and burn.
Do not think I underestimate your great concern.

Ash, ash—
You poke and stir.
75 Flesh, bone, there is nothing there——

A cake of soap,
A wedding ring,
A gold filling.

Herr God, Herr Lucifer
80 Beware
Beware.

Out of the ash
I rise with my red hair
And I eat men like air.

The hills step off into whiteness.
People or stars
Regard me sadly, I disappoint them.

The train leaves a line of breath.
5 O slow
Horse the color of rust,

Hooves, dolorous bells——
All morning the
Morning has been blackening,

10 A flower left out.
My bones hold a stillness, the far
Fields melt my heart.

They threaten
To let me through to a heaven
Starless and fatherless, a dark water.

The woman is perfected.
Her dead

Body wears the smile of accomplishment,
The illusion of a Greek necessity

5   Flows in the scrolls of her toga,
Her bare

Feet seem to be saying:
We have come so far, it is over.

Each dead child coiled, a white serpent,
10   One at each little

Pitcher of milk, now empty.
She has folded

Them back into her body as petals
Of a rose close when the garden

15   Stiffens and odors bleed
From the sweet, deep throats of the night flower.

The moon has nothing to be sad about,
Staring from her hood of bone.

She is used to this sort of thing.
Her blacks crackle and drag.

MARK STRAND

1934–

Born in Summerside, Prince Edward Island, Canada, Mark Strand grew up and attended school in the United States and South America. After graduating from Antioch College, Strand went to Yale and studied painting; in his book *Hopper,* a tribute to the paintings of Edward Hopper, Strand shows himself as a passionate and subtle interpreter of visual art. Strand has written several volumes of poetry and prose, including a book of short stories, *Mr. and Mrs. Baby and Other Stories*. He has also edited several anthologies and translated several poets, including Rafael Alberti and Carlos Drummond de Andrade. A former United States poet laureate, Strand has won the Pulitzer Prize and a MacArthur fellowship.

I don't think anyone is a poet unless they've read other poems.

KEEPING THINGS WHOLE

In a field
I am the absence
of field.
This is
5   always the case.
Wherever I am
I am what is missing.

When I walk
I part the air
10   and always
the air moves in
to fill the spaces
where my body's been.

We all have reasons
15   for moving.
I move
to keep things whole.

Ink runs from the corners of my mouth.
There is no happiness like mine.
I have been eating poetry.

The librarian does not believe what she sees.
Her eyes are sad
and she walks with her hands in her dress.

The poems are gone.
The light is dim.
The dogs are on the basement stairs and coming up.

Their eyeballs roll,
their blond legs burn like brush.
The poor librarian begins to stamp her feet and weep.

She does not understand.
When I get on my knees and lick her hand,
she screams.

I am a new man.
I snarl at her and bark.
I romp with joy in the bookish dark.

MARK STRAND

FOR JESSICA, MY DAUGHTER

Tonight I walked,
close to the house,
and was afraid,
not of the winding course
5   that I have made of love and self
but of the dark and faraway.
I walked, hearing the wind
and feeling the cold,
but what I dwelled on
10   were the stars blazing
in the immense arc of sky.

Jessica, it is so much easier
to think of our lives,
as we move under the brief luster of leaves,
15   loving what we have,
than to think of how it is
such small beings as we
travel in the dark
with no visible way
20   or end in sight.

Yet there were times I remember
under the same sky
when the body's bones became light
and the wound of the skull
opened to receive
the cold rays of the cosmos,
and were, for an instant,
themselves the cosmos,
there were times when I could believe
we were the children of stars
and our words were made of the same
dust that flames in space,
times when I could feel in the lightness of breath
the weight of a whole day
come to rest.

But tonight
it is different.
Afraid of the dark
in which we drift or vanish altogether,
I imagine a light
that would not let us stray too far apart,
a secret moon or mirror,
a sheet of paper,
something you could carry
in the dark
when I am away.

MARK STRAND

What of the neighborhood homes awash
In a silver light, of children hunched in the bushes,
Watching the grown-ups for signs of surrender,
Signs that the irregular pleasures of moving
From day to day, of being adrift on the swell of duty,
Have run their course? Oh parents, confess
To your little ones the night is a long way off
And your taste for the mundane grows; tell them
Your worship of household chores has barely begun;
Describe the beauty of shovels and rakes, brooms and mops;
Say there will always be cooking and cleaning to do,
That one thing leads to another, which leads to another;
Explain that you live between two great darks, the first
With an ending, the second without one, that the luckiest
Thing is having been born, that you live in a blur
Of hours and days, months and years, and believe
It has meaning, despite the occasional fear
You are slipping away with nothing completed, nothing
To prove you existed. Tell the children to come inside,
That your search goes on for something you lost—a name,
A family album that fell from its own small matter
Into another, a piece of the dark that might have been yours,
You don't really know. Say that each of you tries
To keep busy, learning to lean down close and hear
The careless breathing of earth and feel its available
Languor come over you, wave after wave, sending
Small tremors of love through your brief,
Undeniable selves, into your days, and beyond.

Not every man knows what he shall sing at the end,
Watching the pier as the ship sails away, or what it will seem like
When he's held by the sea's roar, motionless, there at the end,
Or what he shall hope for once it is clear that he'll never go back.

5   When the time has passed to prune the rose or caress the cat,
When the sunset torching the lawn and the full moon icing it down
No longer appear, not every man knows what he'll discover instead.
When the weight of the past leans against nothing, and the sky

Is no more than remembered light, and the stories of cirrus
10 And cumulus come to a close, and all the birds are suspended in flight,
Not every man knows what is waiting for him, or what he shall sing
When the ship he is on slips into darkness, there at the end.

MARK STRAND

THE NIGHT, THE PORCH

To stare at nothing is to learn by heart
What all of us will be swept into, and baring oneself
To the wind is feeling the ungraspable somewhere close by.
Trees can sway or be still. Day or night can be what they wish.
5   What we desire, more than a season or weather, is the comfort
Of being strangers, at least to ourselves. This is the crux
Of the matter, which is why even now we seem to be waiting
For something whose appearance would be its vanishing—
The sound, say, of a few leaves falling, or just one leaf,
10   Or less. There is no end to what we can learn. The book out there
Tells us as much, and was never written with us in mind.

RICHARD BRAUTIGAN

1935–1984

Much of Richard Brautigan's life, from his birthplace to his apparent suicide, remains full of mystery and rumor. In 1955, having never published a poem or attended college, he moved to San Francisco, where he became part of the beat scene. His first poem was published in 1956. Brautigan remained little known until the publication of *Trout Fishing in America* (1967), a novel that received widespread critical and popular acclaim. In 1968, he created *Please Plant This Book,* a collection of eight poems printed on the backs of seed packets. He also championed the idea of libraries where people could leave their unpublished works for others to read.

I wrote poetry for seven years to learn how to write a sentence because I really wanted to write novels and I couldn't write a novel until I could write a sentence. I used poetry as a lover but I never made her my old lady.

ORANGES

Oh, how perfect death
computes an orange wind
that glows from your footsteps,

and you stop to die in
5   an orchard where the harvest
fills the stars.

FOR EMMETT

Death is a beautiful car parked only
to be stolen on a street lined with trees
whose branches are like the intestines
    of an emerald.

5 You hotwire death, get in, and drive away
like a flag made from a thousand burning
    funeral parlors.

You have stolen death because you're bored.
There's nothing good playing at the movies
10   in San Francisco.

You joyride around for a while listening
to the radio, and then abandon death, walk
away, and leave death for the police
    to find.

A BASEBALL GAME

Baudelaire went
to a baseball game
and bought a hot dog
and lit up a pipe
5   of opium.
The New York Yankees
were playing
the Detroit Tigers.
In the fourth inning
10   an angel committed
suicide by jumping
off a low cloud.
The angel landed
on second base,
15   causing the
whole infield
to crack like
a huge mirror.
The game was
20   called on
account of
fear.

I think something beautiful
and amusing is gained
by remembering Sidney Greenstreet,
but it is a fragile thing.

5 The hand picks up a glass.
The eye looks at the glass
and then hand, glass and eye
  fall away.

MARGE PIERCY

1936–

A prolific writer, Marge Piercy has written fourteen books of poetry and fifteen novels, as well as literary essays and social commentary. Piercy's writing is often political, with a strong commitment to feminism, Judaism, environmentalism, and social justice. In the late 1960s, after earning her first recognition as a writer, Piercy dedicated the majority of her time to political activism, including work with the Students for a Democratic Society (SDS). She is currently the poetry editor of *Lilith*.

I am conscious in my poems of exploring the experiences
of being a woman in this society. I am consciously a feminist
working with, by, and for other women.

FOR THE YOUNG WHO WANT TO

Talent is what they say
you have after the novel
is published and favorably
reviewed. Beforehand what
you have is a tedious
delusion, a hobby like knitting.

Work is what you have done
after the play is produced
and the audience claps.
Before that friends keep asking
when you are planning to go
out and get a job.

Genius is what they know you
had after the third volume
of remarkable poems. Earlier
they accuse you of withdrawing,
ask why you don't have a baby,
call you a bum.

The reason people want M.F.A.'s,
take workshops with fancy names
when all you can really
learn is a few techniques,
typing instructions and somebody else's mannerisms

25   is that every artist lacks
a license to hang on the wall
like your optician, your vet
proving you may be a clumsy sadist
whose fillings fall into the stew
30   but you're certified a dentist.

The real writer is one
who really writes. Talent
is an invention like phlogiston
after the fact of fire.
35   Work is its own cure. You have to
like it better than being loved.

The first white hair coils in my hand,
more wire than down.
Out of the bathroom mirror it glittered at me.
I plucked it, feeling thirty creep in my joints,
5   and found it silver. It does not melt.

My twentieth birthday lean as glass
spring vacation I stayed in the college town
twanging misery's electric banjo offkey.
I wanted to inject love right into the veins
10   of my thigh and wake up visible:
to vibrate color
like the minerals in stones under black light.
My best friend went home without loaning me money.
Hunger was all of the time the taste of my mouth.

15   Now I am ripened and sag a little from my spine.
More than most I have been the same ragged self
in all colors of luck dripping and dry,
yet love has nested in me and gradually eaten
those sense organs I used to feel with.
20   I have eaten my hunger soft and my ghost grows stronger.

Gradually, I am turning to chalk,
to humus, to pages and pages of paper,
to fine silver wire like something a violin
could be strung with, or somebody garroted,
25   or current run through: silver truly,
this hair, shiny and purposeful as forceps
if I knew how to use it.

The skyscrapers are dancing by the river,
they are leaping over their reflections
their lightning bright zigzag and beady reflections
jagged and shattered on East River.
5   With voices shrill as children's whistles they hop
while the safes pop open like corn
and the files come whizzing through the air
to snow on the streets that lie throbbing,
eels copulating in heaps.
10   Ticker tape hangs in garlands from the wagging streetlamps.
Standard Oil and General Foods have amalgamated
and Dupont, Schenley and AT&T lie down together.
It does not matter, don't hope, it does not matter.
In the morning the buildings stand smooth and shaven
15   and straight
and all goes on whirring and ticking.
Money is reticulated and stronger than steel or stone or vision,
though sometimes at night
the skyscrapers bow and lean and leap under no moon.

MARGE PIERCY

Full in the hand, heavy
with ripeness, perfume spreading
its fan: moments now resemble
sweet russet pears glowing
5   on the bough, peaches warm
from the afternoon sun, amber
and juicy, flesh that can
make you drunk.

There is a turn in things
10   that makes the heart catch.
We are ripening, all the hard
green grasping, the stony will
swelling into sweetness, the acid
and sugar in balance, the sun
15   stored as energy that is pleasure
and pleasure that is energy.

Whatever happens, whatever,
we say, and hold hard and let
go and go on. In the perfect
20   moment the future coils,
a tree inside a pit. Take,
eat, we are each other's
perfection, the wine of our
mouths is sweet and heavy.
25   Soon enough comes the vinegar.
The fruit is ripe for the taking
and we take. There is
no other wisdom.

This girlchild was born as usual
and presented dolls that did pee-pee
and miniature GE stoves and irons
and wee lipsticks the color of cherry candy.
5 Then in the magic of puberty, a classmate said:
You have a great big nose and fat legs.

She was healthy, tested intelligent,
possessed strong arms and back,
abundant sexual drive and manual dexterity.
10 She went to and fro apologizing.
Everyone saw a fat nose on thick legs.

She was advised to play coy,
exhorted to come on hearty,
exercise, diet, smile and wheedle.
15 Her good nature wore out
like a fan belt.
So she cut off her nose and her legs
and offered them up.

In the casket displayed on satin she lay
20 with the undertaker's cosmetics painted on,
a turned-up putty nose,
dressed in a pink and white nightie.
Doesn't she look pretty? everyone said.
Consummation at last.
To every woman a happy ending.

MICHAEL S. HARPER

1938–

A professor at Brown University, Michael Harper has published more than ten books of poetry, and he has also edited or coedited several anthologies of African and African American poetry. Harper's poems tend to combine national and personal history in unexpected ways. He has written a great deal of poetry about jazz and jazz musicians, infusing his poems with an improvisatory energy and restless spirit reminiscent of saxophonist John Coltrane, about whom he has written often.

In the beginning I never found poems in the American literary pantheon about the things I knew best. I decided that I would at least do my part and try to put some of those poems in there.

Moon child:
March is coming,
In mixed anger,
To an eventual end.
5   The trees have cracked
Under the weight of ice,
Blotting power lines,
And we have been without light,
Days, nights, together.
10   Elms are first to bloom,
Slowly, in fear of constant
Virus, that, heedless,
Will kill them off in ten years;
This year they bloom.
15   The spindly trees,
Taking shape, resist
The inlet, hornet,
And salt-night air.
In this ribald quiet,
20   Revisited without shame,
There is evidence,
Ornate, and our hunger.

No one's been told
that black men
went first to the moon
the dark side

5   for dark brothers
without space ship
gravity complex
in our computer centers
government campuses

10   instant play and replay
white mice and pig-guineas
in concentric digital rows.

Someone has been
pulling brother's curls

15   into fancy barbed wire,
measuring his forelegs,
caressing his dense innards
into formaldehyde
pruning the jellied marrow:

20   a certain formula is appearing:
someone has been studying you.

MICHAEL S. HARPER

THE DANCE OF THE ELEPHANTS

PART 1

The trains ran through the eleven
nights it took to vacate the town;
relatives and lovers tacked in a row
on the button-board sidings,
wails of children tossed in a pile
wails of women tossed in a salad
to be eaten with soap and a rinse.
Those who took all they had to the borders,
those who took their bottles
three centuries old, those who
thought only of language, the written
word, are forgiven.
One daughter is riding on the train
above her mother, above her mother,
into the tunnel of the elephants.

Culture tells us most about its animals
singing our children asleep, or let them
slip into a room as smoothly as
refrigeration.

PART 2

20 To be comforted by Swiss music
is a toy elephant in a box,
skimming the nickelplated air.
Beethoven's a passion dance
forgotten in a stamped coin—
25 *it is magic—it is magic—*

We dance the old beast round the fireplace,
coal engines fuming in a row,
elephant chimes in a toy rain—
human breath skimming the air.

30 We skim the air—
*it is magic—*the engines
smelling the chimes.
Beethoven chiming the magic—
we escape it on a train.

35 Sung in America,
the song some telescopic sight,
a nickelplated cream,
a small girl cuddles her elephant,
the song in the streets
40 leaping the train windows,
and what love as the elephant chimes.

MICHAEL S. HARPER

WE ASSUME: ON THE DEATH OF OUR SON,
REUBEN MASAI HARPER

We assume
that in 28 hours,
lived in a collapsible isolette,
you learned to accept pure oxygen

5   as the natural sky;
the scant shallow breaths
that filled those hours
cannot, did not make you fly—
but dreams were there

10   like crooked palmprints on
the twin-thick windows of the nursery—
in the glands of your mother.

We assume
the sterile hands

15   drank chemicals in and out
from lungs opaque with mucus,
pumped your stomach,
eeked the bicarbonate in
crooked, green-winged veins,

20   out in a plastic mask;

A woman who'd lost her first son
consoled us with an angel gone ahead
to pray for our family—
gone into that sky

25   seeking oxygen,
gone into autopsy,
a fine brown powdered sugar,
a disposable cremation:

We assume
you did not know we loved you.

He's talking about interpolations
riffs that come in the midst

of action, responding to the line,
accommodating the blues

5   and note neglecting the melody
refusing to smother beauty

with too many chords
to show off is to bungle

the melody with chordal blocks
10   not building anything to your baby

hiding the melody
like only the young can do

Lester Young would watch the dancers
moving into his vernaculars

15   with rhythms augmenting the melody
Herschel would set the pace

Pres would follow
Count would comp time

as though you could improve
20   on stride piano

Ben Webster could do stride
when you get possessed with wild chords

tie your left hand behind your back
then play the melody with one finger

25   on your right hand:
put the melody on your heart

FOR RAY BROWN

Miles (being ahead)
came in early

with the sketches
he did not mention Japanese

5   visual art
though Bill Evans did

his liner notes
stretching each brushstroke

as metaphor
10   for playing together

Because you cannot go back
resonance builds

new material
at a recording session

15   only once
in a lifetime

For these players
five settings

and a figure
20   who asked of us

to do this
perfectly

as if to play *live*
alone in a group

25   Miles asked
we answered

         MICHAEL S. HARPER

YUSEF KOMUNYAKAA

1947–

Born in a rural Louisiana town, Yusef Komunyakaa frequently uses his childhood experiences and the rhythms of jazz and blues music to inform his work. The eldest of five children, Komunyakaa did not begin writing until he joined the army directly after high school. He served in Vietnam, earning the Bronze Star for his work on a military newspaper. After leaving the army, he attended the University of Colorado, Colorado State University, and the University of California at Irvine. Komunyakaa has received the Pulitzer Prize and the Thomas Forcade Award for Literature and Art Dedicated to the Healing of Vietnam in America.

Poetry is a kind of distilled insinuation. It's a way of expanding and talking around an idea or a question. Sometimes, more actually gets said through such a technique than a full frontal assault.

Beyond King Ptolemy's dream
outside the broken
girdle of chance, beyond
the Lighthouse of Pharos
5   in a kingdom of sea turtles,
nothing can inter or outrun
a stormy heart. Beyond galleon
& disappearing lovers, a flame
flounces behind a glass crab
10   to signal a craggy reef
in the Bay of Alexandria.
Beyond archipelagos of drizzle
& salt, Armageddon & hellfire,
bearded seals turn into Helen's
15   mermaids sunning on a white beach
beside Paris, where blotches of ink
map omens. Beyond Atlantis
uncovered by desert winds
phantom armies ride against,
20   necklaces of shark's teeth
adorn virgins. When earth
dilates, the known magnifies
till unknowns tincture silk,
till pomegranates bleed
25   redemption into soil.
Sirens cry across dark
waters, as anguelle becomes air,
beyond the mapmaker's omphalos
where hydra first mounted Venus.

If you had asked
after my fifth highball,
as I listened to Miles' midnight
trumpet, in Venus De Milo's embrace,
5 I would have nodded
Yes, as if I didn't
own my tongue. *Yes,*
I believe I am
flesh & fidelity
10 again. I washed lipstick
off the teacup, faced
your photo to the wall,
swept up pieces of goodtime
moshed with dustballs,
15 & haggled with myself
over a bar of lemon soap.
Yes, I could now feel
luck's bile & desire
sweetened by creamy chocolates,
20 & I would have bet
my Willie Mays cards
a strand of your hair
clinging to an old Thelonious T-shirt
could never make me fall apart
25 at this bedroom window
beneath a bloodred moon.

UNTITLED BLUES

AFTER A PHOTOGRAPH BY YEVGENI YEVTUSHENKO

I catch myself trying
to look into the eyes
of the photo, at a black boy
behind a laughing white mask
5 he's painted on. I
could've been that boy
years ago.
Sure, I could say
everything's copacetic,
10 listen to a Buddy Bolden cornet
cry from one of those coffin-
shaped houses called
shotgun. We could
meet in Storyville,
15 famous for quadroons,
with drunks discussing God
around a honky-tonk piano.
We could pretend we can't
see the kitchen help
20 under a cloud of steam.
Other lurid snow jobs:
night & day, the city
clothed in her see-through
French lace, as pigeons
25 coo like a beggar chorus
among makeshift studios
on wheels—Vieux Carré

belles having portraits
painted
twenty years younger.
30   We could hand jive
down on Bourbon & Conti
where tap dancers hold
to their last steps,
mammy dolls frozen
35   in glass cages. The boy
locked inside your camera,
perhaps he's lucky—
he knows how to steal
laughs in a place
40   where your skin
is your passport.

YUSEF KOMUNYAKAA

Two bad actors canonized by ballads
flowering into dusk, crowned with hoarfrost.
But the final blows weren't dealt in Meung-
sur-Loire or the Angola pen. "Irene,
5   Irene, I'll see you in my dreams."

Unmoved by the hangman's leer,
these two roughhouse bards ignored
his finger traveling down the list.
They followed every season's penniless
10   last will & testament. Their songs

bleed together years. A bridge,
more than a ledger of bones.
Ghosts under the skin in bedlam,
Prince of Fools, they prowled
15   syncopated nights of wolfbane

& gin mills of starlight
at The Golden Mortar & The Bucket
of Blood, double-daring men across
thresholds, living down the list,
strung out on immortality's rag.

Put away those insipid spoons.
The frontal lobe horn section went home hours ago.
The trap drum has been kicked
down the fire escape,
5   & the tenor's ballad amputated.
Inspiration packed her bags.
Her caftan recurs in the foggy doorway
like brain damage; the soft piano solo of her walk
evaporates; memory loses her exquisite tongue,
10   looking for "green silk stockings with gold seams"
on a nail over the bathroom mirror.
Tonight I sleep with Silence,
my impossible white wife.

BIRDS ON A POWERLINE

Mama Mary's counting them
Again. Eleven black. A single
Red one like a drop of blood

Against the sky. She's convinced
5   They've been there two weeks.
I bring her another cup of coffee

& a Fig Newton. I sit here reading
Frances Harper at the enamel table
Where I ate teacakes as a boy,

10   My head clear of voices brought back.
The green smell of the low land returns,
Stealing the taste of nitrate.

The deep-winter eyes of the birds
Shine in summer light like agate,
15   As if they could love the heart

Out of any wild thing. I stop,
With my finger on a word, listening.
They're on the powerline, a luminous

Message trailing a phantom
20   Goodyear blimp. I hear her say
Jesus, I promised you. Now

He's home safe, I'm ready.
My traveling shoes on. My teeth
In. I got on clean underwear.

LINDA HOGAN

1947–

A member of the Chickasaw nation, Linda Hogan writes poems that focus on issues of human rights and identity as well as ecological responsibility. She is often described as one of the most provocative and influential Native American figures in American literature. In addition to poetry, Hogan has written essays, fiction, and an award-winning play. At the center of her writing is her belief that in life all things are connected.

I don't believe in such a thing as talent. It takes perseverance.
I will do it over and over again until I get it right.

Nothing sings in our bodies
like breath in a flute.
It dwells in the drum.
I hear it now
5   that slow beat
like when a voice said to the dark,
let there be light,
let there be ocean
and blue fish
10   born of nothing
and they were there.
I turn back to bed.
The man there is breathing.
I touch him
15   with hands already owned by another world.
Look, they are desert,
they are rust. They have washed the dead.
They have washed the just born.
They are open.
20   They offer nothing.
Take it.
Take nothing from me.
There is still a little life
left inside this body,
25   a little wildness here
and mercy
and it is the emptiness
we love, touch, enter in one another
and try to fill.

I dream my fingers are knives
I open
like a deck of cards
and read sunlight on the blades.

5 Two of Hearts,
born to a world of weapons.
Even your bones are knives
like the hands your neighbors conceal
with their glint of finger blades
10 clattering against tin spoons.

You would think
these hands that save birds,
hands that feed dogs
and heal the broken leg of a crane,
15 you would think the hands that love,
the Two of Hearts,
were always gentle.

Every morning
they turn back the quilt.
20 They offer cornmeal to the sun.
They brush hair.
These hands are full of God.

But I never forget
to recite history,
25 to recall the entire world
and all the young men
who became sergeants
with terror

LINDA HOGAN

disguised in their soft, loving hands,
30 the hands that hold hands with death,
and I am their blood,
no matter what,
and I am not their blood,
no matter,
35 but, oh, this world,
this cut and cutting world.

TWO

The weight of a man on a woman
is like falling into the river without drowning.

Above, the world is burning and fighting.
Lost worlds flow through others.

5   But down here beneath water's skin,
river floor, sand, everything

is floating, rocking.
Water falls through our hands as we fall through it.

And when a woman and a man come up from water
10   they stand at the elemental edge of difference.

Mirrored on water's skin,
they are fired clay, water evaporating into air.

They are where water turns away from land
and goes back to enter a larger sea.

15   A man and a woman are like those rivers,
entering a larger sea

greater than the sum of all its parts.

The floorboards creak.
The moon is on the wrong side of the building,

and burns remain
on the floor.

5   The house wants to fall down
the universe when earth turns.

It still holds the coughs of old men
and their canes tapping on the floor.

I think of Indian people here before me
10   and how last spring white merchants hung an elder

on a meathook and beat him
and he was one of The People.

I remember this war
and all the wars

15   and relocation like putting the moon in prison
with no food and that moon already a crescent,

but be warned, the moon grows full again
and the roofs of this town are all red

and we are looking through the walls of houses
20   at people suspended in air.

Some are baking, with flour on their hands,
or sleeping on floor three, or getting drunk.

I see the businessmen who hit their wives
and the men who are tender fathers.

25 There are women crying or making jokes.
Children are laughing under beds.

Girls in navy blue robes talk on the phone all night
and some Pawnee is singing 49s, drumming the table.

Inside the walls
30 world changes are planned, bosses overthrown.

If we had no coffee,
cigarettes, or liquor,

says the woman in room twelve,
they'd have a revolution on their hands.

35 Beyond walls are lakes and plains,
canyons and the universe;

the stars are the key
turning in the lock of the night.

Turn the deadbolt and I am home.
40 I have walked dark earth,

opened a door to nights where there are no apartments,
just drumming and singing;

The Duck Song, The Snake Song,
The Drunk Song.

45 No one here remembers the city
or has ever lost the will to go on.

Hello aunt, hello brothers, hello trees
and deer walking quietly on the soft red earth.

CELEBRATION: BIRTH OF A COLT

When we reach the field
she is still eating
the heads of yellow flowers
and pollen has turned her whiskers
5   gold. Lady,
her stomach bulges out,
the ribs have grown wide.
We wait, our bare feet dangling
in the horse trough,
10   warm water
where goldfish brush
our smooth ankles.
We wait
while the liquid breaks
15   down Lady's dark legs
and that slick wet colt
like a black tadpole
darts out
beginning at once
20   to sprout legs.
She licks it to its feet,
the membrane still there,
red,
transparent
25   the sun coming up shines through,
the sky turns bright with morning
and the land
with pollen blowing off the corn,
land that will always own us,
everywhere it is red.

RAY A. YOUNG BEAR

1950–

A member of the Meskwaki (People of the Red Earth) nation of Native Americans, Ray Young Bear grew up on settlement land, where he still lives. He and his wife, Stella, are cofounders of a performance group that tours the country, preserving Native American culture through readings, drumming, and songs. Young Bear's first language is Meskwaki; he did not begin writing in English until high school. Robert Bly was an early mentor, and Young Bear's poetry is kindred to Bly's, expressing a profound understanding of the natural world and its inhabitants.

For me, writing is a personal link to the writings of my grandfathers. I have in my possession their journals that date back to the early 1800s. I therefore believe that "word-collecting" is genetically encoded in my blood.

In the blizzard
while chopping wood
the mystical whistler
beckons my attention.
5   Once there were longhouses
here. A village.
In the abrupt spring floods
swimmers retrieved our belief.
Their spirit remains.
10   From the spotted night
distant jets transform
into fireflies who float
towards me like incandescent
snowflakes.
15   The leather shirt
which is suspended
on a wire hanger
above the bed's headboard
is humanless; yet when one
20   stands outside the house,
the strenuous sounds
of dressers and boxes
being moved can be heard.
We believe someone wears
25   the shirt and rearranges
the heavy furniture,
although nothing
is actually changed.
Unlike the Plains Indian shirts
30   which repelled lead bullets,
ricocheting from them
in fiery sparks,
this shirt is the means;
this shirt *is* the bullet.

Last night when the yellow moon
of November broke through the last line
of turbulent Midwestern clouds,
a lone frog, the same one
5   who probably announced
the premature spring floods,
attempted to sing.
Veterans' Day, and it was
sore-throat weather.
10   In reality the invisible musician
reminded me of my own doubt.
The knowledge that my grandfathers
were singers as well as composers—
one of whom felt the simple utterance
15   of a vowel made for the start
of a melody—did not produce
the necessary memory or feeling
to make a Wadasa Nakamoon,
Veterans' Song.
20   All I could think of
was the absence of my name
on a distant black rock.
Without this monument
I felt I would not be here.
25   For a moment, I questioned
why I had to immerse myself
in country, controversy and guilt,
but I wanted to honor them.
Surely, the song they presently
30   listened to along with my grandfathers
was the ethereal kind which did not stop.

RAY A. YOUNG BEAR

An immature black eagle walks assuredly
across a prairie meadow. He pauses in mid-step
with one talon over the wet snow to turn
around and see.

5   Imprinted in the tall grass behind him
are the shadows of his tracks,
claws instead of talons, the kind
that belong to a massive bear.
And he goes by that name:
10   *Me kwi so ta.*

And so this aegis looms against the last
spring blizzard. We discover he's concerned
and the white feathers of his spotted hat
flicker, signaling this.

15   With outstretched wings he tests the sutures.
Even he is subject to physical wounds and human
tragedy, he tells us.

The eyes of the Bear-King radiate through
the thick, falling snow. He meditates the loss
20   of my younger brother—and by custom
suppresses his emotions.

It is the thunderstorm
        at first
that begins speaking
        from an easterly direction
5   We listen to its vociferous
        non-threatening
voice and fall asleep

This weather doesn't care
        to know itself
10 our inner physical journals
record

We assess: icy rain is no different
        than wet branch-breaking
snow and the summer deluge
15   that stretches
toward autumn combines all into one
        haunting answer

that of a wintry inevitability
        glazed ice
20 over the terrain
        The symphony

Before awakening we hear clouds
that quietly explode
        from within
25 Watery moonlit fragments hit
        the roof
        saying: in the case of anger
fist-sized hail would splinter
        everything

RAY A. YOUNG BEAR

30 The woodlands horizon
is therefore portrayed as a jagged
    lavender line
and encircled in yellow
        obviously
35 is the sun
        reducing humankind
to spherical dimensions
        making
known the presence
40 of duality

That the Black Hummingbirds
are saviours as well as
assassins

        ∽

Grandmother Earth
45 sits with her bare razor-nicked
back towards you
        the observer
the would-be infringer
        the one who taps out
50 salvation messages with a silver
surgical instrument

Her daughter's precious son
                    she recognizes
But the blood-letting is deceptive
55   What was supposed
                              to be seasonal
self-purification appears through
                    ultrasound
as a protoplasmic thorn
60   carved with indecipherable
                              petroglyphs

                    ॰

We swear nothing is apocalyptic
while garish beacons from
                    the tribal gaming complex
65   create apparitions
in the sky

Balanced on a floating mass
                    of ourselves and
under the guidance of an ochre
70   seal-eyed
word-collector in a tight
flannel shirt
                    hole-ridden jeans
and Presbyterian church–donated
75   shoes
we cradle fine shovels
that are designed to slice
                    the earth
leaving behind rectangular-
80   shaped markings
of a former industrious
society

RAY A. YOUNG BEAR

RITA DOVE

1952–

One of the youngest poets ever to win the Pulitzer Prize, Rita Dove is also the youngest person to be named poet laureate of the United States, a position she held for two terms. In addition to poetry, Dove has published short fiction, novels, and a verse play. There is in much of her poetry a complex examination of American history and the challenges of family life.

In writing a poem, if the reader on the other end can come up and say: "I know what you meant, I mean, I felt that too"—then we are a little less alone in the world, and that to me is worth an awful lot.

TESTIMONIAL

Back when the earth was new
and heaven just a whisper,
back when the names of things
hadn't had time to stick;

5   back when the smallest breezes
melted summer into autumn,
when all the poplars quivered
sweetly in rank and file . . .

the world called, and I answered.
10   Each glance ignited to a gaze.
I caught my breath and called that life,
swooned between spoonfuls of lemon sorbet.

I was pirouette and flourish,
I was filigree and flame.
15   How could I count my blessings
when I didn't know their names?

Back when everything was still to come,
luck leaked out everywhere.
I gave my promise to the world,
and the world followed me here.

How she sat there,
the time right inside a place
so wrong it was ready.

That trim name with
5 its dream of a bench
to rest on. Her sensible coat.

Doing nothing was the doing:
the clean flame of her gaze
carved by a camera flash.

10 How she stood up
when they bent down to retrieve
her purse. That courtesy.

In the old neighborhood, each funeral parlor
is more elaborate than the last.
The alleys smell of cops, pistols bumping their thighs,
each chamber steeled with a slim blue bullet.

5   Low-rent balconies stacked to the sky.
A boy plays tic-tac-toe on a moon
crossed by TV antennae, dreams

he has swallowed a blue bean.
It takes root in his gut, sprouts
10   and twines upward, the vines curling
around the sockets and locking them shut.

And this sky, knotting like a dark tie?
The patroller, disinterested, holds all the beans.

August. The mums nod past, each a prickly heart on a sleeve.

Swing low so I
can step inside—
a humming ship of voices
big with all

5   the wrongs done
done them.
No sound this generous
could fail:

ride joy until
10   it cracks like an egg,
make sorrow
seethe and whisper.

From a fortress
of animal misery
15   soars the chill voice
of the tenor, enraptured

with sacrifice.
What do I see,
he complains, notes
20   brightly rising

towards a sky
blank with promise.
Yet how healthy
the single contralto

NAOMI SHIHAB NYE

1952–

Born in St. Louis, Missouri, to a Palestinian father and an American mother, Naomi Shihab Nye received her bachelor's degree from Trinity University in San Antonio, Texas, where she still lives. Nye has traveled in the Middle East and lived in Jerusalem, and she often explores the complexity of the Palestinian experience in her poems. In addition to writing poetry, Nye has edited several anthologies of both poetry and prose and written books for children.

Probably some of us were taught so long and hard that poetry was a thing to analyze that we lost our ability to find it delicious, to appreciate its taste, sometimes even when we couldn't completely apprehend its meaning.

MINNOWS

All night I stare into the mirror
at the deep wrinkle beginning to show
on my forehead above the right eye.

I move the muscles of my face
5   to see where it comes from
and it comes from everywhere,
pain, joy, the look of being puzzled
and raising one eyebrow,
from the way I say YES too much,
10   I say YES when I mean NO
and the wrinkle grows.

It is cutting a line across my head
like a crack in a creek bottom—
starting small, shiver between two stones,
15   it ends up splitting the bed.

I wade carefully, feeling with feet—
smooth-skinned pebbles,
the minnow's effortless glide.

For other fruits my father was indifferent.
He'd point at the cherry trees and say,
"See those? I wish they were figs."
In the evenings he sat by my bed
5   weaving folktales like vivid little scarves.
They always involved a figtree.
Even when it didn't fit, he'd stick it in.
Once Joha was walking down the road and he saw a figtree.
Or, he tied his camel to a figtree and went to sleep.
10 Or, later when they caught and arrested him,
his pockets were full of figs.

At age six I ate a dried fig and shrugged.
"That's not what I'm talking about!" he said,
"I'm talking about a fig straight from the earth—
15 gift of Allah!— on a branch so heavy it touches the ground.
I'm talking about picking the largest fattest sweetest fig
in the world and putting it in my mouth."
(Here he'd stop and close his eyes.)

Years passed, we lived in many houses, none had figtrees.
20 We had lima beans, zucchini, parsley, beets.
"Plant one!" my mother said, but my father never did.
He tended garden half-heartedly, forgot to water,
let the okra get too big.
"What a dreamer he is. Look how many things he starts
25 and doesn't finish."

The last time he moved, I got a phone call.
My father, in Arabic, chanting a song I'd never heard.
"What's that?"
"Wait till you see!"

NAOMI SHIHAB NYE

30 He took me out to the new yard.
 There, in the middle of Dallas, Texas,
 a tree with the largest, fattest, sweetest figs in the world.
 "It's a figtree song!" he said,
 plucking his fruits like ripe tokens,
35 emblems, assurance
 of a world that was always his own.

Why do your poems comfort me, I ask myself.
Because they are upright, like straight-backed chairs.
I can sit in them and study the world as if it too
were simple and upright.

5   Because sometimes I live in a hurricane of words
and not one of them can save me.
Your poems come in like a raft, logs tied together,
they float.
I want to tell you about the afternoon
10   I floated on your poems
all the way from Durango Street to Broadway.

Fathers were paddling on the river with their small sons.
Three Mexican boys chased each other outside the library.
Everyone seemed to have some task, some occupation,
15   while I wandered uselessly in the streets I claim to love.

Suddenly I felt the precise body of your poems beneath me,
like a raft, I felt words as something portable again,
a cup, a newspaper, a pin.
Everything happening had a light around it,
20   not the light of Catholic miracles,
the blunt light of a Saturday afternoon.
Light in a world that rushes forward with us or without us.
I wanted to stop and gather up the blocks behind me
in this light, but it doesn't work.
25   You keep walking, lifting one foot, then the other,
saying "This is what I need to remember"
and then hoping you can.

NAOMI SHIHAB NYE

November   November   November   the days crowd together
like families of leaves   in a dry field
I pick up a round stone   take it to my father
who lies in bed waiting for his heart to mend
5   and he turns it over and over in his hands

My father is writing me the story of his village
He tells what people did   in another country
before I was born   how his best friend was buried alive
and the boy survived two days in the ground
10   how my father was lowered into a well on ropes   to discover
clay jars a thousand years old   how each jar held seeds
carob and melon   and the villagers chose secrecy
knowing the British would come with trucks and dig up their town

My father's handwriting changes from page to page
15   sometimes wild scrawl and disconnected letters
sometimes a new serious upward slant

And me   I travel the old roads again and again
wearing a different life in a house surrounded by trees
At night the dropping pecans make little clicks above us
20   Doors closing

More and more I understand what people do
I appreciate the daily braveries   clean white shirts
morning greetings between old men

Again I see how   once the boat tips   you never forget
25   the sensation of drowning
even if you sing yourself the familiar songs

Today my face is stone   my eyes are buckets
I walk the streets lowering them into everything
but they come up empty

30   I would tell my father
        I cannot move one block without you
        I will never recover from your love
yet I stand by his bed saying things I have said before
and he answers   and we go on this way
35   smoothing the silences
nothing can heal

NAOMI SHIHAB NYE

BLOOD

"A true Arab knows how to catch a fly in his hands,"
my father would say. And he'd prove it,
cupping the buzzer instantly
while the host with the swatter stared.

5 In the spring our palms peeled like snakes.
True Arabs believed watermelon could heal fifty ways.
I changed these to fit the occasion.

Years before, a girl knocked,
wanted to see the Arab.
10 I said we didn't have one.
After that, my father told me who he was,
"Shihab"—"shooting star"—
a good name, borrowed from the sky.
Once I said, "When we die, we give it back?"
15 He said that's what a true Arab would say.

Today the headlines clot in my blood.
A little Palestinian dangles a truck on the front page.
Homeless fig, this tragedy with a terrible root
is too big for us. What flag can we wave?
20 I wave the flag of stone and seed,
table mat stitched in blue.

I call my father, we talk around the news.
It is too much for him,
neither of his two languages can reach it.
25 I drive into the country to find sheep, cows,
to plead with the air:
Who calls anyone *civilized*?
Where can the crying heart graze?
What does a true Arab do now?

Choose one word and say it over
and over, till it builds a fire inside your mouth.
Adhafera, the one who holds out, *Alphard,* solitary one,
the stars were named by people like us.
Each night they line up on the long path between worlds.
They nod and blink, no right or wrong
in their yellow eyes. *Dirah,* little house,
unfold your walls and take us in.

My well went dry, my grandfather's grapes
have stopped singing. I stir the coals,
my babies cry. How will I teach them
they belong to the stars?
They build forts of white stone and say, "This is mine."
How will I teach them to love *Mizar,* veil, cloak,
to know that behind it an ancient man
is fanning a flame?
He stirs the dark wind of our breath.
He says the veil will rise
till they see us shining, spreading like embers
on the blessed hills.

Well, I made that up. I'm not so sure about *Mizar.*
But I know we need to keep warm here on earth
and when your shawl is as thin as mine is, you tell stories.

NAOMI SHIHAB NYE

GARY SOTO

1952–

Gary Soto was born in Fresno, California. He has written poems and stories for both adults and children, as well as a libretto and literary criticism. Soto's narrators take up the issues of the urban barrio, the migrant worker, and the tenant farmer, searching the present and the past for their Chicano identity and spiritual origins. Whether hip and streetwise or gritty and hard, the language of Soto's poetry is witty, incisive, and filled with political passion.

For me, the joy of being a writer is to take things I see and hear and then rearrange them.

Remember that you are moving away   sister
From what was a summer
Of hunger
And of thorns deep in your feet
5   Prayers that unraveled
Like mama's stockings
At the day's end
When she came back from candling eggs

Those small things you knew on the old street
10   Have vanished   a holly bush
And its bright jays
The rocks you scratched
From the yard
And were your dolls   blond dolls
15   Given heartbeats   names   legs
The sighs of those
About to cry
                 Remember that you have left
Grandpa nodding like a tall weed
20   Over his patch of chilies and tomatoes
Left a jar of secrets
Buried in the vacant lot
On a hot day
And our family some distance
25   From your life
Remember

In the mid-sixties
We were sentenced to watch
The rich on TV—Donna Reed
High-heeled in the kitchen,
5   Ozzie Nelson bending
In his eighth season, over golf.
While he swung, we hoed
Fields flagged with cotton
Because we understood a sock
10   Should have a foot,
A cuff a wrist,
And a cup was always
Smaller than the thirst.
When Donna turned
15   The steak and onions,
We turned grape trays
In a vineyard
That we worked like an abacus,
A row at a time.

20   And today the world
Still plots, unravels with
Piano lessons for this child,
Braces for that one—
Gin in the afternoon,
25   Ice from the bucket . . .
But if the electricity
Fails, in this town,
A storefront might

GARY SOTO

Be smashed, sacks may find
30   Hands, a whistle
Point the way.
And if someone steps out
With a black and white TV,
It's because we love you Donna,
We miss you Ozzie.

At eight I was brilliant with my body.
In July, that ring of heat
We all jumped through, I sat in the bleachers
Of Romain Playground, in the lengthening
Shade that rose from our dirty feet.
The game before us was more than baseball.
It was a figure—Hector Moreno
Quick and hard with turned muscles,
His crouch the one I assumed before an altar
Of worn baseball cards, in my room.

I came here because I was Mexican, a stick
Of brown light in love with those
Who could do it—the triple and hard slide,
The gloves eating balls into double plays.
What could I do with fifty pounds, my shyness,
My black torch of hair, about to go out?
Father was dead, his face no longer
Hanging over the table or our sleep,
And mother was the terror of mouths
Twisting hurt by butter knives.

In the bleachers I was brilliant with my body,
Waving players in and stomping my feet,
Growing sweaty in the presence of white shirts.
I chewed sunflower seeds. I drank water
And bit my arm through the late innings.
When Hector lined balls into deep
Center, in my mind I rounded the bases
With him, my face flared, my hair lifting
Beautifully, because we were coming home
To the arms of brown people.

GARY SOTO

At ten I wanted fame. I had a comb
And two Coke bottles, a tube of Brylcreem.
I borrowed a dog, one with
Mismatched eyes and a happy tongue,
5   And wanted to prove I was tough
In the alley, kicking over trash cans,
A dull chime of tuna cans falling.
I hurled light bulbs like grenades
And men teachers held their heads,
10   Fingers of blood lengthening
On the ground. I flicked rocks at cats,
Their goofy faces spurred with foxtails.
I kicked fences. I shooed pigeons.
I broke a branch from a flowering peach
15   And frightened ants with a stream of spit.
I said *"Chale,"* "In your face," and "No way
Daddy-O" to an imaginary priest
Until grandma came into the alley,
Her apron flapping in a breeze,
20   Her hair mussed, and said, "Let me help you,"
And punched me between the eyes.

At twenty, John Berryman raised a fountain pen
And flicked ink on paper. At the same age,
Under the Fresno sun, I told myself,
I could get fifty bucks for my Rambler.
5   The car had killed three stripeless cats
And splattered a grille of butterflies.
I thought of Berryman and my dead car.
The radiator leaked in two places,
Biblical wounds that made me touch my palms.
10   The windshield was cracked
Like Henry James's bowl. The torn car seat
Was a gag of cotton.
Here was Jarrell on the crushed front fender,
And here was Twain's muddy river circling
15   From engine block to radiator.
Here was a matchbook with Bukowski's telephone number.
Here was a crushed can on the floorboard,
And the bottle cap of its metallic sweetness.
Here was Edgar Lee Masters,
20   His grassy eyebrows poking around a tree.
Here was a wise-ass junior with four English classes.
I was selling my slave ship.
The radio was gone, the visor pelted with dust,
The grille like a flat-nosed shark.
25   I drove up the street
Past the yards hanging with fruit,
Plum that was the blood of Christ, grape
That the fox ate employing only his front teeth.
I drove to a junkyard,
30   Where fifty was really thirty-five,
A big seed in overalls licking his thumb
And counting them out in greasy fives.

GARY SOTO

His dog peed on my car tire and barked inches
From my crotch. I waved good-bye
35 And the walk home took two hours. Black birds
Pecked at glass and sand. A stinky wind
From the cement works dusted my nose,
And three rednecks stopped their Ford Pinto
To push me around. I walked through the heat
40 That was nothing like Moses sneaking from Egypt.
Upper division English didn't help.
It was hell itself, Mr. Dante,
Not a spiral into the earth but a flat march home.

JANE HIRSHFIELD

1953–

In addition to being a poet, Jane Hirshfield is a translator of Asian poetry and the editor of *Women in Praise of the Sacred*, an anthology of women's spiritual writing. Her life and writings convey a deep regard for the natural world and its creatures, emphasizing the importance in poetry of an ethical relationship between imagination and image. Zen Buddhism is central to Hirshfield's life, as demonstrated by her three-year hiatus from writing to concentrate on meditation and study.

I have never thought of poems as "art," but as life: reading a good poem is as integral to my life's course as any other experience. For the part of us that is sponge, poems are water, and a living sponge is inseparable from what it has taken in.

FOR WHAT BINDS US

There are names for what binds us:
strong forces, weak forces.
Look around, you can see them:
the skin that forms in a half-empty cup,

5   nails rusting into the places they join,
joints dovetailed on their own weight.
The way things stay so solidly
wherever they've been set down—
and gravity, scientists say, is weak.

10   And see how the flesh grows back
across a wound, with a great vehemence,
more strong
than the simple, untested surface before.
There's a name for it on horses,

15   when it comes back darker and raised: proud flesh,

as all flesh
is proud of its wounds, wears them
as honors given out after battle,
small triumphs pinned to the chest—

20   And when two people have loved each other
see how it is like a
scar between their bodies,
stronger, darker, and proud;
how the black cord makes of them a single fabric
that nothing can tear or mend.

Under
a thin coat of dust
dull globes
of pomegranates
5   ripen.

No easy fruit,
these sweet-seeded
leatherskinned
puckering
10   moons
that clench
& pull the brushwood
closer to ground—

Wild branches
15   interweave
into a thickening idiom
of wood:

muttered polysyllabic of twig,
guttural patois
20   of leaf
in a green-belled dusk,
and the vowels, slurred,
hanging
in drunken heat.

25   *Yes,* they say (that sweetness
in the mouth mixing with pith,
a difficult promise
made once to a dark King),
yes, I will return everything.

Because I know tomorrow
his faithful gelding heart will be broken
when the spotted mare is trailered and driven away,
I come today to take him for a gallop on Diaz ridge.

5 Returning, he will whinny for his love.
Ancient, spavined,
her white parts red with hill-dust,
her red parts whitened with the same, she never answers.

But today, when I turn him loose at the bent gate
10 with the taste of chewed oat on his tongue
and the saddle-sweat rinsed off with water,
I know he will canter, however tired,
whinnying wildly up the ridge's near side,
and I know he will find her.

15 He will be filled with the sureness of horses
whose bellies are grain-filled,
whose long-ribbed loneliness
can be scratched into no-longer-lonely.

His long teeth on her withers,
20 her rough-coated spots will grow damp and wild.
Her long teeth on his withers,
his oiled-teakwood smoothness will grow damp and wild.
Their shadows' chiasmus will fleck and fill with flies,
the eight marks of their fortune stamp and then cancel the earth.
25 From ear-flick to tail-switch, they stand in one body.
No luck is as boundless as theirs.

The heart's reasons
seen clearly,
even the hardest
will carry
5   its whip-marks and sadness
and must be forgiven.

As the drought-starved
eland forgives
the drought-starved lion
10   who finally takes her,
enters willingly then
the life she cannot refuse,
and is lion, is fed,
and does not remember the other.

15   So few grains of happiness
measured against all the dark
and still the scales balance.

The world asks of us
only the strength we have and we give it.
Then it asks more, and we give it.

The rain falling too lightly to shape
an audible house, an audible tree,
blind, soaking, the old horse waits in his pasture.

He knows the field for exactly what it is:
5   his limitless mare, his beloved.
Even the mallards sleep in her red body maned
in thistles, hooved in the new green shallows of spring.

Slow rain streams from fetlocks, hips, the lowered head,
while she stands in the place beside him that no one sees.

10   The muzzles almost touch.
How silently the heart pivots on its hinge.

As the house of a person
in age sometimes grows cluttered
with what is
too loved or too heavy to part with,
5   the heart may grow cluttered.
And still the house will be emptied,
and still the heart.

As the thoughts of a person
in age sometimes grow sparer,
10   like a great cleanness come into a room,
the soul may grow sparer;
one sparrow song carves it completely.
And still the room is full,
and still the heart.

15   Empty and filled,
like the curling half-light of morning,
in which everything is still possible and so why not.

Filled and empty,
like the curling half-light of evening,
20   in which everything now is finished and so why not.

Beloved, what can be, what was,
will be taken from us.
I have disappointed.
I am sorry. I knew no better.

25   A root seeks water.
Tenderness only breaks open the earth.
This morning, out the window,
the deer stood like a blessing, then vanished.

JANE HIRSHFIELD

HOPE AND LOVE

All winter
the blue heron
slept among the horses.
I do not know
5   the custom of herons,
do not know
if the solitary habit
is their way,
or if he listened for
10   some missing one—
not knowing even
that was what he did—
in the blowing
sounds in the dark.
15   I know that
hope is the hardest
love we carry.
He slept
with his long neck
20   folded, like a letter
put away.

I have envied those
who make something
useful, sturdy—
a chair, a pair of boots.

5   Even a soup,
rich with potatoes and cream.

Or those who fix, perhaps,
a leaking window:
strip out the old cracked putty,
10   lay down cleanly the line of the new.

You could learn,
the mirror tells me, late at night,
but lacks conviction.
One reflected eyebrow quivers a little.

15   I look at this
borrowed apartment—
everywhere I question it,
the wallpaper's pattern matches.

Yesterday a woman
20   showed me
a building shaped
like the overturned hull of a ship,

its roof trusses, under the plaster,
lashed with soaked rawhide,
25   the columns' marble
painted to seem like wood.
Though possibly it was the other way around?

I look at my unhandy hand,
innocent,
shaped as the hands of others are shaped.
Even the pen it holds is a mystery, really.

Rawhide, it writes,
and *chair,* and *marble.*
Eyebrow.

Later the woman asked me—
I recognized her then,
my sister, my own young self—

Does a poem enlarge the world,
or only our idea of the world?

How do you take one from the other,
I lied, or did not lie,
in answer.

MARTÍN ESPADA

1957–

In addition to being a poet, Martín Espada is an English professor and a lawyer. He is a strong proponent of Puerto Rican independence, and his writing is frequently historical in subject matter and political in tone. In 1997, National Public Radio commissioned Espada to write a poem for National Poetry Month. Espada chose as his subject the journalist Mumia Abu-Jamal, jailed after a controversial conviction for killing a police officer. NPR, involved in a lawsuit with Abu-Jamal, refused to air the poem.

I think that a poet can be a historian, just as a poet can be a sociologist or journalist or teacher or organizer.

BULLY

In the school auditorium,
the Theodore Roosevelt statue
is nostalgic
for the Spanish-American war,
5   each fist lonely for a saber
or the reins of anguish-eyed horses,
or a podium to clatter with speeches
glorying in the malaria of conquest.

But now the Roosevelt school
10   is pronounced Hernández.
Puerto Rico has invaded Roosevelt
with its army of Spanish-singing children
in the hallways,
brown children devouring
15   the stockpiles of the cafeteria,
children painting Taíno ancestors
that leap naked across murals.

Roosevelt is surrounded
by all the faces
20   he ever shoved in eugenic spite
and cursed as mongrels, skin of one race,
hair and cheekbones of another.

Once Marines tramped
from the newsreel of his imagination;
25   now children plot to spray graffiti
in parrot-brilliant colors
across the Victorian mustache
and monocle.

No one asks
where I am from,
I must be
from the country of janitors,
I have always mopped this floor.
Honduras, you are a squatter's camp
outside the city
of their understanding.

No one can speak
my name,
I host the fiesta
of the bathroom,
stirring the toilet
like a punchbowl.
The Spanish music of my name
is lost
when the guests complain
about toilet paper.

What they say
must be true:
I am smart,
but I have a bad attitude.

No one knows
that I quit tonight,
maybe the mop
will push on without me,
sniffing along the floor
like a crazy squid
with stringy gray tentacles.
They will call it Jorge.

MARTÍN ESPADA

THE LOVER OF A SUBVERSIVE IS ALSO A SUBVERSIVE

The lover of a subversive
is also a subversive.
The painter's compañero was a conspirator,
revolutionary convicted
5   to haunt the catacombs of federal prison
for the next half century.
When she painted her canvas
on the beach, the FBI man
squatted behind her
10   on the sand, muddying his dark gray suit
and kissing his walkie-talkie,
a pallbearer who missed
the funeral train.

The painter who paints a subversive
15   is also a subversive.
In her portrait of him, she imagines
his long black twist of hair. In her portraits
of herself, she wears a mask
or has no mouth. She must sell the canvases,
20   for the FBI man ministered solemnly
to the principal at the school
where she once taught.

The woman who grieves for a subversive
is also a subversive.
25 The FBI man is a pale-skinned apparition
staring in the subway.
She could reach for him
and only touch a pillar of ash
where the dark gray suit had been.
30 If she hungers to touch her lover,
she must brush her fingers
on moist canvas.

The lover of a subversive
is also a subversive.
35 When the beach chilled cold,
and the bright stumble of tourists
deserted, she and the FBI man
were left alone with their spying glances,
as he waited calmly
40 for the sobbing to begin,
and she refused to sob.

FIDEL IN OHIO

The bus driver tore my ticket
and gestured at the tabloid
spread across the steering wheel.
The headline:

5   FIDEL CASTRO DEAD
REPLACED BY IDENTICAL DOUBLE
Below, two photographs of Fidel,
one with cigar, one without.

"The resemblance is amazing,"
10   the driver said,
and I agreed.

"Yes, Your Honor, there are rodents,"
said the landlord to the judge,
"but I let the tenant
have a cat. Besides,
he stacks his tires
in the hallway."

The tenant confessed
in stuttering English:
"Yes, Your Honor,
I am from El Salvador,
and I put my tires
in the hallway."

The judge puffed up
his robes
like a black bird
shaking off rain:
"Tires out of the hallway!
You don't live in a jungle
anymore. This
is a civilized country."

So the defendant was ordered
to remove his tires
from the hallways of civilization,
and allowed to keep the cat.

MARTÍN ESPADA

At sixteen, I worked after high school hours
at a printing plant
that manufactured legal pads:
Yellow paper
5   stacked seven feet high
and leaning
as I slipped cardboard
between the pages,
then brushed red glue
10   up and down the stack.
No gloves: fingertips required
for the perfection of paper,
smoothing the exact rectangle.
Sluggish by 9 P.M., the hands
15   would slide along suddenly sharp paper,
and gather slits thinner than the crevices
of the skin, hidden.
Then the glue would sting,
hands oozing
20   till both palms burned
at the punchclock.

Ten years later, in law school,
I knew that every legal pad
was glued with the sting of hidden cuts,
25   that every open lawbook
was a pair of hands
upturned and burning.

Every night
the ex–mental patient,
forgetful of the medicine
that caused him to forget,
5   would climb to the roof
of the transient hotel
with a flashlight,
waiting for his Martian parents
and their spaceship,
10 flashlight beam waving
like the baton of a conductor
firm in the faith
that this orchestra
will one night
give him music.

MARTÍN ESPADA

LI-YOUNG LEE

1957−

Born in Jakarta, Indonesia, to Chinese parents, Li-Young Lee and his family came to the United States in 1964. Lee has written several award-winning poems and books of poetry. His work is equally influenced by Asian and American traditions and contains a deeply spiritual element. Family, too, is a dominant theme, especially explorations of his complex relationship with his father.

I'm highly aware that I'm a guest in the language. I'm wondering if that's not the truth for all of us.

THE GIFT

To pull the metal splinter from my palm
my father recited a story in a low voice.
I watched his lovely face and not the blade.
Before the story ended, he'd removed
5 the iron sliver I thought I'd die from.

I can't remember the tale,
but hear his voice still, a well
of dark water, a prayer.
And I recall his hands,
10 two measures of tenderness
he laid against my face,
the flames of discipline
he raised above my head.

Had you entered that afternoon
15 you would have thought you saw a man
planting something in a boy's palm,
a silver tear, a tiny flame.
Had you followed that boy
you would have arrived here,
20 where I bend over my wife's right hand.

Look how I shave her thumbnail down
so carefully she feels no pain.
Watch as I lift the splinter out.
I was seven when my father
took my hand like this,
and I did not hold that shard
between my fingers and think,
Metal that will bury me,
christen it Little Assassin,
Ore Going Deep for My Heart.
And I did not lift up my wound and cry,
Death visited here!
I did what a child does
when he's given something to keep.
I kissed my father.

EARLY IN THE MORNING

While the long grain is softening
in the water, gurgling
over a low stove flame, before
the salted Winter Vegetable is sliced
5   for breakfast, before the birds,
my mother glides an ivory comb
through her hair, heavy
and black as calligrapher's ink.

She sits at the foot of the bed.
10   My father watches, listens for
the music of comb
against hair.

My mother combs,
pulls her hair back
15   tight, rolls it
around two fingers, pins it
in a bun to the back of her head.
For half a hundred years she has done this.
My father likes to see it like this.
20   He says it is kempt.

But I know
it is because of the way
my mother's hair falls
when he pulls the pins out.
25   Easily, like the curtains
when they untie them in the evening.

I've pulled the last of the year's young onions.
The garden is bare now. The ground is cold,
brown and old. What is left of the day flames
in the maples at the corner of my
5 eye. I turn, a cardinal vanishes.
By the cellar door, I wash the onions,
then drink from the icy metal spigot.

Once, years back, I walked beside my father
among the windfall pears. I can't recall
10 our words. We may have strolled in silence. But
I still see him bend that way—left hand braced
on knee, creaky—to lift and hold to my
eye a rotten pear. In it, a hornet
spun crazily, glazed in slow, glistening juice.

15 It was my father I saw this morning
waving to me from the trees. I almost
called to him, until I came close enough
to see the shovel, leaning where I had
left it, in the flickering, deep green shade.

20 White rice steaming, almost done. Sweet green peas
fried in onions. Shrimp braised in sesame
oil and garlic. And my own loneliness.
What more could I, a young man, want.

EATING TOGETHER

In the steamer is the trout
seasoned with slivers of ginger,
two sprigs of green onion, and sesame oil.
We shall eat it with rice for lunch,
brothers, sister, my mother who will
taste the sweetest meat of the head,
holding it between her fingers
deftly, the way my father did
weeks ago. Then he lay down
to sleep like a snow-covered road
winding through pines older than him,
without any travelers, and lonely for no one.

Lie still now
while I prepare for my future,
certain hard days ahead,
when I'll need what I know so clearly this moment.

5   I am making use
of the one thing I learned
of all the things my father tried to teach me:
the art of memory.

I am letting this room
10   and everything in it
stand for my ideas about love
and its difficulties.

I'll let your love-cries,
those spacious notes
15   of a moment ago,
stand for distance.

Your scent,
that scent
of spice and a wound,
20   I'll let stand for mystery.

Your sunken belly
is the daily cup
of milk I drank
as a boy before morning prayer.

25   The sun on the face
of the wall
is God, the face
I can't see, my soul,

and so on, each thing
30 standing for a separate idea,
and those ideas forming the constellation
of my greater idea.
And one day, when I need
to tell myself something intelligent
35 about love,

I'll close my eyes
and recall this room and everything in it:
My body is estrangement.
This desire, perfection.
40 Your closed eyes my extinction.
Now I've forgotten my
idea. The book
on the windowsill, riffled by wind . . .
the even-numbered pages are
45 the past, the odd-
numbered pages, the future.
The sun is
God, your body is milk . . .

useless, useless . . .
50 your cries are song, my body's not me . . .
no good . . . my idea
has evaporated . . . your hair is time, your thighs are song . . .
it had something to do
with death . . . it had something
to do with love.

Tonight my brother, in heavy boots, is walking
through bare rooms over my head,
opening and closing doors.
What could he be looking for in an empty house?
5   What could he possibly need there in heaven?
Does he remember his earth, his birthplace set to torches?
His love for me feels like spilled water
running back to its vessel.

At this hour, what is dead is restless
10   and what is living is burning.

Someone tell him he should sleep now.

My father keeps a light on by our bed
and readies for our journey.
He mends ten holes in the knees
15   of five pairs of boy's pants.
His love for me is like his sewing:
various colors and too much thread,
the stitching uneven. But the needle pierces
clean through with each stroke of his hand.

20   At this hour, what is dead is worried
and what is living is fugitive.

Someone tell him he should sleep now.
God, that old furnace, keeps talking
with his mouth of teeth,
25   a beard stained at feasts, and his breath
of gasoline, airplane, human ash.
His love for me feels like fire,
feels like doves, feels like river-water.

At this hour, what is dead is helpless, kind

30   and helpless. While the Lord lives.

Someone tell the Lord to leave me alone.
I've had enough of his love
that feels like burning and flight and running away.

GERRY CRINNIN

1958–

A former navy journalist, Gerry Crinnin is now an associate professor of English at Jamestown Community College in New York. His poems often draw on his experiences growing up in upstate New York and working as a disc jockey for Armed Services Radio in Antarctica. Crinnin's poetry blends vivid phrasing with a romantic sense of human possibility. His chapbooks include *Loveletter in Smithereens* and *Bullfrog Pants from the Estranged Grove.*

A perfect stranger once said to me: "Writers are important because they create new places for people to live." Then he disappeared. Poems are like that—startling and true, then gone, but remembered, reconstructed—like cubicles, nests, flowering fields and, in some cases, the moon.

NOCTURNE

I drifted to the beach in the black evening summer
and the warm blue. It was the hour of perfume in the mouth
and the moon, abandoned, full of teeth.

Dealing out the haul of dreams
5   night still remains
in the hands of a few.

I, for one, hold on to you.

Is the diction
of all pebbles on the beach
correct and clear?

Have I checked the moon
to see if
there's a comma?

Is all the punctuation
euphonious as
haberdasher?

Have I avoided eternity
a notch or two?

Does my theme contain an old
dirty dress, a large green bug
settled on the torn leaf?

COMMON GRAVE

It's mercy to know
no one'll ever know
who I really was
or am

5   Nor say a lot about
what I ever thought about
what made me talk in
my own time

Save a space for me
10   in space for me
put a marble there
or stone

That was me and
that was me and
I called them home

Last night, last evening
When you became very tall in the dying
Down of engines and wind
Did you speak with that young girl
5 Of our lives?
Leaf, and the last bird breaking
The heart of the ocean?

Did she arrive?

Put it away, cast it off,
10 The thought of leaving every woman
In the sweet hours,
And settle here: twilight, cold winds,
Snow and a frequent moon, nothing
To nobody, a good man.

A NOTE ON METER

Part of what makes poetry different from other kinds of writing is its compact and vivid means of expression. In fact, in ancient times, poetry served as a way to put important information into a form of language that people could easily memorize, because written language did not yet exist. Lines that rhyme or that have a definite sequence of sound and stress are easier to remember than lines without these patterns. Two of the most obvious formal qualities of poetry are therefore rhyme and *meter*, or the pattern of accents in a poem.

Consider these famous opening lines from Robert Frost's poem "Stopping by Woods on a Snowy Evening": "Whose woods these are I think I know. / His house is in the village though." The rhyme is obvious and the meter compelling. By the time you've said "His house is in the village," you feel the poem demanding one more word, of exactly one syllable and rhyming with "know." Critics of this poem find its forceful rhythm—they might call it a singsong rhythm—too strong, but a great deal of poetry throughout history has had this kind of compelling formal structure because that's what makes poems easy to remember. Before the development of written language, people "published" family histories, stories of battles and wars, and even things like classic recipes by putting them into poems that were, like Robert Frost's poem, hard to forget.

Rhythm and Meter

So much in nature is rhythmical. Whether we speak of the march of the seasons, the repetition of day and night, or the movements of electrons and light waves, the things of this world move in a rhythmical dance. It is the same with language. Even our everyday speech, which is not consciously organized into rhythmical forms, shifts in and out of patterns. Poetry is often rhythmical in any number of ways. This rhythm is organized in different ways and to varying degrees. Even when we speak of free verse, we are not necessarily speaking of language that is "free" of orchestrated rhythmical effects.

Three ways to organize the rhythm of a line are (1) by syllable, (2) by accent, and (3) by meter. Meter is the most complicated, and in some ways a combination of the other two.

SYLLABIC AND ACCENTUAL VERSE

Look at this poem:

TRIAD

These be
Three silent things:
The falling snow. . the hour
Before the dawn. . the mouth of one
Just dead.

Notice how the lines build in length until the close. Now count the syllables in each line. This poem is a *cinquain,* which is a five-line poem consisting of two, four, six, eight, and two syllables respectively. Adelaide Crapsey invented the cinquain, and "Triad" is her most famous rendering of the form.

In *syllabic* verse, such as "Triad," the number of syllables in each line determines the identity of the line. There needn't be the same number of syllables in every line. Instead, a pattern of the poet's choosing carries through the poem. Haiku is the most familiar example of syllabic poetry. The conventional Western interpretation of haiku consists of three lines, with five, then seven, then five syllables.

MAYO
CLINIC

PLUMMER PROJECT

Ramona Wills
100 Village View Circle
Apt 111
Williamsburg Iowa 52361

Looser kinds of syllabic verse are also possible. John Logan often writes in lines alternating between seven and thirteen syllables, as in these lines from "Poem for My Brother":

Blue's my older brother's color. Mine is brown, you see.
So today I bought this ring
of gold and lapis lazuli flecked with a bright bronze.

Poetry written with a fixed number of accents or stresses in each line is called *accentual* verse. Some of the earliest Old English poetry was accentual, with a four-stress line generally separated into two halves by a pause, or *caesura*. Even though the number of accents remains the same from line to line in accentual verse, the pattern of accents and the number of unaccented syllables can change as the poem proceeds. In the following lines from "Ash-Wednesday," T. S. Eliot uses a two-stress line but varies the number of unstressed syllables:

　　/　　　/
Lady of silences

　　/　　　　/
Calm and distressed

　　/　　　　　/
Torn and most whole

　　/　　　/
Rose of memory

　　/　　　　/
Rose of forgetfulness

　　/　　　　/
Exhausted and life-giving

　　/　　　　/
Worried reposeful

Poets often experiment with accentual patterns. Look at "The Red Wheelbarrow," by William Carlos Williams:

so much depends
upon

a red wheel
barrow

glazed with rain
water

beside the white
chickens

In each stanza, the accentual pattern is two stresses, then one. In addition, the second line of each stanza is always two syllables. The first lines—as we see just by looking at the poem—are close to the same length. The poem is in fact symmetrical: 4/2, 3/2, 3/2, 4/2. Because symmetry is pattern, one could argue that this poem is syllabic as well as accentual.

METER

That time of year thou mayst in me behold
When yellow leaves, or none, or few, do hang
Upon those boughs which shake against the cold,
Bare ruined choirs where late the sweet birds sang.

In this passage from Shakespeare's sonnet 73, we have the most complex organization of rhythm possible: meter. Meter is the combination of syllable count and accentual pattern into a musical system. This type of meter is based on a tradition that goes back at least to the ancient Greeks, from whom we derive our terminology.

According to this system, there are several different rhythmical patterns, each consisting of two or three syllables. These patterns are called *feet*. This term can be distracting at first, given the familiarity of the word. But if you consider that what we are doing is *measuring* a line of poetry, the term seems to fit better.

In English poetry, you will find four standard types of feet. Each contains one accented and one or two unaccented syllables:

SYMBOLS

1. **Iamb** (iambic): An unaccented syllable followed by an accented syllable. ⌣ ╱

2. **Trochee** (trochaic): An accented syllable followed by an unaccented syllable. ╱ ⌣

3. **Anapest** (anapestic): Two unaccented syllables followed by an accented syllable. ⌣ ⌣ ╱

4. **Dactyl** (dactylic): An accented syllable followed by two unaccented syllables. ╱ ⌣ ⌣

You might also hear of the *pyrrhic* foot, which has two unaccented syllables, and the *spondaic* foot or *spondee*, which has two accented syllables. The ancient Greeks measured their feet of these same names as "long" and "short" according to the duration of the vowels. Because English has no equivalent for measuring duration, but rather measures stress, it is difficult to imagine feet with no accents or, to a lesser degree, feet with two equally accented syllables.

A metric line is measured and named according to the number of feet it has:

Monometer:	one foot
Dimeter:	two feet
Trimeter:	three feet
Tetrameter:	four feet

Pentameter:	five feet
Hexameter:	six feet
Heptameter:	seven feet
Octameter:	eight feet

A line that consists predominantly of iambs (some feet may vary) and contains five total feet is called *iambic pentameter*. The vast majority of English metrical poetry is iambic. And if you look at everyday speech, you'll notice that it, too, frequently falls into iambic patterns. Pentameter is also the most widely used line length that you'll encounter, turning up in the poems of such diverse poets as William Shakespeare, John Milton, John Keats, Percy Bysshe Shelley, and the contemporary poets Robert Frost, Wallace Stevens, and Donald Hall. You might wonder, why pentameter? Poet Mary Oliver suggests that our English-language breath capacity is about that long. Of course the amount of breath that a ten-syllable line can take is quite variable; nevertheless, it seems likely that we have a physiological preference for pentameter.

HOW TO SCAN A POEM

For many years, the study of poetry placed great emphasis on a poem's meter. *Scansion*, or the analysis of a poem's metrical structure, was king. Today, most of the study of poetry centers on a poem's meaning. Somewhere between these two approaches lies the ideal middle ground, where the meaning of a poem's words is made more intense, more memorable, and more significant by an understanding of the poem's formal structure.

Try this exercise: Read a poem, preferably aloud, with a conscious effort to notice the syllables. Count the syllables in several lines. Is there a number that seems to be the most common, or around which all the line counts distribute themselves? If yes, that would suggest a metrical poem, or perhaps, depending on the regularity of the results, a syllabic poem.

Let's assume that there is no *absolutely* regular syllable count, or that there is enough variation to rule out a syllabic poem. If, say, the average or most common result is ten syllables, then test for iambic pentameter, which would be five feet of iambic rhythm. Statistics are with you in this assumption because, as we've already noted, iambic pentameter is the most widely used meter in English metrical poetry.

Now pick any line that has the average number of syllables (ten), because it stands a good chance of being a relatively easy line to scan. For example, it is unlikely to have trisyllabic feet or *truncated* (abbreviated or incomplete) feet. Next, divide the ten syllables by pairs with vertical lines. Don't worry about splitting up words or having more than one foot within a single word. It happens. When you are scanning a poem, the line is no more than a sequence of syllables, so word identity isn't an issue.

These divisions mark the five feet in the line. Presumably most are iambs, but as many as two or even three could be substitutions. A *substitution* is any type of foot other than the predominant one. In an iambic poem, for example, trochees are the most common substitution, and you might find anapests or even dactyls as well. Read your line aloud naturally, noting where the vocal stresses fall. Vocal stress and metrical accent often coincide, so a reading should point out some of the "high points" in the meter. Where the difference between a vocally unstressed and stressed syllable is great, we have what we might call a "strong" accent. Where the difference is slight, we may have two strong stresses or, conversely, two weak vocal stresses. Remember that, either way, each foot by definition must contain one metrical accent. Either two strong or two weak stresses may turn out to be an iamb.

Now go through the line foot by foot, determining which syllable is accented. Keep in mind that iambs will be the most common, and that grammar often determines the pattern of accents. The natural tendency in speech is to give some sounds more weight than others. Usually, a word's contextual and grammatical importance affects where the stress will fall. We tend to stress verbs and nouns much more often than prepositions, conjunctions, articles, or even adjectives and adverbs. The action in a sentence, or the subjects and objects of a sentence, are usually of primary importance, and we indicate this importance by vocal stress. And vocal stress often—but not always—coincides with metrical accent. Lastly, trust your ear. If you relax and listen to yourself read, you'll start to hear where the accents fall.

In any given poem, some lines will be relatively easy to scan. Let's take a close look at the opening line of Shakespeare's sonnet 73, for example:

> That time of year thou mayst in me behold

Ten syllables, right? Well, "mayst" may give you pause for a moment, but consider the spelling. Despite the hack pronunciation of Elizabethan English that is prevalent as parody or in error, we can tell that the word is one syllable for the simple reason that there is no second vowel. Dividing the ten syllables into pairs is then simple:

> That time | of year | thou mayst | in me | behold

The accented syllables in most of these feet are easy enough to determine. "Behold" is the easiest, and in scansion you don't need to start at the beginning of the line—just jump in wherever you can find a grip. The scanned line, when spoken with the appropriate accents, looks like this:

> ˘ ´ ˘ ´ ˘ ´ ˘ ´ ˘ ´
> That time | of year | thou mayst | in me | behold

Keep in mind that if you find a variation in the meter, it is not some sort of mistake, an indication that Shakespeare just couldn't pull it off. Staying perfectly in meter is not the point. Do you judge drummers by the machinelike precision of their beat and shake your head whenever they leave the beat and play a drum-and-cymbal fill? Of course not. That's what makes drumming exciting: the anticipation of how the expected beat can be wonderfully varied. The same applies to meter. Variation is the essence of humanity. A computer can keep a great beat. Drummers these days often play to a click track, which keeps perfect time. But we still have drummers, because we love the dynamics of change.

In metrical poetry, moreover, the changes are not always variation for its own sake. A change in the meter often highlights a significant passage in the poem. Students frequently ask, did the poet do that on purpose? There's no easy answer to that question. Does every artist intend every nuance of meaning we receive? And is it a defect in the art if meaning is not purposeful? No and no, we would contend. By a process strange and wonderful, the emotional or meaningful highlights in a line, like large boulders in a stream, cause "ripples" in the flow of words. And so as attentive readers we can, by feeling the "ripples," often sense the most complex passages in a poem. Scansion therefore is more than measuring, more than a simple surveying of the poetic landscape. It helps us see beneath the surface as well.

alliteration The repetition of identical or nearly identical sounds at the beginning of consecutive or nearby words. The term is usually applied only to consonants.

> EXAMPLE: from "FOR A YOUNG ARTIST," Robert Hayden
>
> Carloads of the curious paid
> his clever hosts to see the
> actual angel? carny freak?
> in the barbedwire pen.
>
> A poet looks not only for the perfect word or phrase to convey an image, but also for complementary sounds.

allusion A reference to a historical or fictional person, place, thing, or event, or to another literary work that suggests a wider frame of reference or greater depth of meaning.

> EXAMPLE: "OUT, OUT—," Robert Frost (p. 82)
>
> Frost's title makes reference to a speech on the fleeting nature of life by Macbeth in Shakespeare's *Macbeth*. How do the events of the poem relate to the allusion Frost makes?

apostrophe A direct address to an object, an abstraction, or an absent or deceased person.

> EXAMPLE: "TO MY DEAD FATHER," Frank O'Hara (p. 309)

assonance The repetition of similar vowel sounds in nearby words.

> EXAMPLE: from "POEM, SLOW TO COME, ON THE DEATH OF CUMMINGS (1894–1962)," John Logan
>
> Summer blasts the roots of trees and weeds
> again, and you are dead
> almost a year. I am sorry for my fear,
>
> In this example, the assonance of "trees" and "weeds" creates an approximate or **slant rhyme**.

connotation and **denotation** *Connotation* refers to the ideas and feelings commonly associated with or suggested by a word. *Denotation* is the dictionary definition of a word.

> **EXAMPLE:** from "FROM THE MISERY OF DON JOOST," Wallace Stevens
>
> I have finished my combat with the sun;
> And my body, the old animal,
> Knows nothing more.
>
> What is the denotation of *combat?* Of *animal?* What are the connotations?

elegy A poem composed as a formal and sustained lament on the death of a particular person.

> **EXAMPLE:** "OH MAX," Robert Creeley (p. 284)

euphony Language that is pleasant and harmonious to the ear.

> **EXAMPLE:** from "LEGEND," Hart Crane
>
> As silent as a mirror is believed
> Realities plunge in silence by . . .

hyperbole A figure of speech that uses exaggeration for emphasis or effect and can also reveal aspects of a character or situation that are not directly stated.

> **EXAMPLE:** from "JORGE THE CHURCH JANITOR FINALLY QUITS," Martín Espada
>
> No one asks
> where I am from,
> I must be
> from the country of janitors,
>
> What does this exaggeration tell us about the speaker of the poem?

image and **imagery** An *image* is a visual representation of a thought, feeling, or sense impression. *Imagery* refers to all of these sensory details, both literal and figurative, in a poem or other work of literature.

> **EXAMPLE:** from "MY GRANDMOTHER'S LOVE LETTERS," Hart Crane
>
> There are no stars to-night
> But those of memory.
> Yet how much room for memory there is
> In the loose girdle of soft rain.

metaphor A figure of speech that involves an implied or direct comparison between two unlike things.

> **EXAMPLE:** from "TO WAKEN AN OLD LADY," William Carlos Williams

> Old age is
> a flight of small
> cheeping birds
> skimming
> bare trees
> above a snow glaze.

personification A figure of speech in which human characteristics are assigned to nonhuman things.

> **EXAMPLE:** from "RHAPSODY ON A WINDY NIGHT," T. S. Eliot

> Half-past one,
> The street-lamp sputtered,
> The street-lamp muttered,
> The street-lamp said, "Regard that woman

refrain A line, phrase, or group of lines that is repeated in a poem.

> **EXAMPLE:** "NOTICE WHAT THIS POEM IS NOT DOING," William Stafford (p. 225)

> How does the repetition of the title phrase influence the reading and inter-pretation of the poem? This refrain is used five times. Is it the timing or the phrase that is important?

rhythm The pattern of accents or stresses in lines of poetry.

> **EXAMPLE:** from "ACQUAINTED WITH THE NIGHT," Robert Frost

> I have been one acquainted with the night.
> I have walked out in rain—and back in rain.
> I have outwalked the furthest city light.

> Read these lines aloud and notice the consistency of the rhythm.

satire A literary work that uses irony, sarcasm, or wit to expose the absurdity of life or human nature.

> **EXAMPLE:** "AMERICAN GOTHIC," William Stafford (p. 226)

> The title suggests a satirical view of American values. What is Stafford saying about the view through "tiny,/grim glasses"?

simile A comparison between two unlike things using the word *like* or *as*.

> **EXAMPLE:** from "THE SUBVERTED FLOWER," Robert Frost
>
> Though with every word he spoke
> His lips were sucked and blown
> And the effort made him choke
> Like a tiger at a bone.

slant rhyme A partial or inexact rhyme, often using assonance or consonance only.

> **EXAMPLE:** from "MY SON MY EXECUTIONER," Donald Hall
>
> My son, my executioner,
>   I take you in my arms,
> Quiet and small and just astir
>   And whom my body warms.

style The particular characteristics of an author's writing as achieved through word choice, syntax, kinds of figurative language, form, and theme.

symbol A word, phrase, or image that is itself and also stands for something else.

> **EXAMPLE:** "QUEEN-ANNE'S-LACE," William Carlos Williams (p. 108)

theme A central idea in a literary work.

tone The attitude or feeling that pervades a given work, as determined by word choice, style, imagery, connotation, sound, and rhythm.

> **EXAMPLE:** "THREE PRESIDENTS," Robert Bly (p. 266)
>
> How and why does the tone in this poem change in moving from one president to the next?

All possible care has been taken to trace ownership and secure permission for each selection in this anthology. The Great Books Foundation wishes to thank the following authors, publishers, and representatives for permission to reprint copyrighted material:

Elizabeth Bishop: *Chemin de Fer; The Fish; Invitation to Miss Marianne Moore; Sestina; Insomnia; Sandpiper;* and *North Haven,* from THE COMPLETE POEMS, 1927–1979, by Elizabeth Bishop. Copyright 1979, 1983, by Alice Helen Methfessel. Reprinted by permission of Farrar, Straus, and Giroux, LLC.

Robert Bly: *Three Presidents; After Long Busyness; The Dead Seal; In Rainy September; Why We Don't Die;* and *Things to Think,* from EATING THE HONEY OF WORDS, by Robert Bly. Copyright 1999 by Robert Bly. Reprinted by permission of HarperCollins Publishers, Inc.

Richard Brautigan: *Oranges; Death Is a Beautiful Car Parked Only; A Baseball Game;* and *The Sidney Greenstreet Blues,* from THE PILL VERSUS THE SPRINGHILL MINE DISASTER, by Richard Brautigan. Copyright 1965 by Richard Brautigan, renewed 1993 by Ianthe Brautigan Swensen. Reprinted by permission of Houghton Mifflin Company. All rights reserved.

Gwendolyn Brooks: *The preacher: ruminates behind the sermon; The sonnet-ballad; We Real Cool;* and *To Black Women,* from SELECTED POEMS, by Gwendolyn Brooks. Copyright 1994 by The Estate of Gwendolyn Brooks. Reprinted by permission of The Estate of Gwendolyn Brooks.

Hart Crane: *Legend; My Grandmother's Love Letters; Garden Abstract; Chaplinesque;* and *Recitative,* from COMPLETE POEMS OF HART CRANE, by Hart Crane, edited by Marc Simon. Copyright 1933, 1958, 1966 by Liveright Publishing Corporation. Copyright 1986 by Marc Simon. Reprinted by permission of Liveright Publishing Corporation.

Robert Creeley: *The Innocence; I Know a Man; The Rain;* and *The Language,* from COLLECTED POEMS OF ROBERT CREELEY, 1945–1975, by Robert Creeley. Copyright 1983 by the Regents of the University of California. Reprinted by permission of the Regents of the University of California and the University of California Press. *Arroyo* and *This Day,* from LATER, by Robert Creeley. Copyright 1979 by Robert Creeley. Reprinted by permission of New Directions Publishing Corporation. *Self-Portrait; If Happiness;* and *Oh Max,* from MIRRORS, by Robert Creeley. Copyright 1983 by Robert Creeley. Reprinted by permission of New Directions Publishing Corporation.

Gerry Crinnin: *Nocturne; Final Exam; Common Grave;* and *Walking Through Glass,* by Gerry Crinnin. Printed by permission of the author.

E. E. Cummings: *Five Americans;* [because it's/Spring]; [a great/man]; [who are you,little i]; [Buffalo Bill 's/defunct]; [if there are any heavens my mother will(all by herself)have]; [somewhere i have never travelled,gladly beyond]; [at dusk/just when]; and [l(a/le/af], from COMPLETE POEMS, 1904–1962, by E. E. Cummings, edited by George J. Firmage. Copyright 1923, 1925, 1926, 1931, 1935, 1938, 1939, 1940, 1944, 1945, 1946, 1947, 1948, 1949, 1950, 1951, 1952, 1953, 1954, 1955, 1956, 1957, 1958, 1959, 1960, 1961, 1962, 1963, 1966, 1967, 1968, 1972, 1973, 1974, 1975, 1976, 1977, 1978, 1979, 1980, 1981, 1982, 1983, 1984, 1985, 1986, 1987, 1988, 1989, 1990, 1991 by the Trustees for the E. E. Cummings Trust. Copyright 1973, 1976, 1978, 1979, 1981, 1983, 1985, 1991 by George James Firmage. Reprinted by permission of Liveright Publishing Corporation.

Emily Dickinson: [I taste a liquor never brewed]; [I'm Nobody! Who are you?]; [I felt a Funeral, in my Brain]; [This World is not conclusion]; [The Soul selects her own Society]; [I died for Beauty - but was scarce]; [I heard a Fly buzz - when I died]; [Undue Significance a starving man attaches]; and [Perception of an Object costs], from THE POEMS OF EMILY DICKINSON, READING EDITION, by Emily Dickinson, edited by R. W. Franklin. Copyright 1914, 1918, 1919, 1924, 1929, 1930, 1932, 1935, 1937, 1942 by Martha Dickinson Bianchi. Copyright 1951, 1955, 1979 by the President and Fellows of Harvard College. Copyright 1952, 1957, 1958, 1963, 1965 by Mary L. Hampson. Copyright 1998, 1999 by the President and Fellows of Harvard College. Reprinted by permission of the Belknap Press of Harvard University Press and the Trustees of Amherst College.

H. D.: *The Helmsman; Chance; Fragment 113; Lethe;* and *Leda,* from COLLECTED POEMS, 1912–1944, by Hilda Doolittle. Copyright 1982 by The Estate of Hilda Doolittle. Reprinted by permission of New Directions Publishing Corporation.

Rita Dove: *Testimonial* and *Rosa,* from ON THE BUS WITH ROSA PARKS, by Rita Dove. Copyright 1999 by Rita Dove. Reprinted by permission of W. W. Norton & Company, Inc. *"Teach Us to Number Our Days"* and *Gospel,* from SELECTED POEMS, by Rita Dove. Copyright 1980, 1986 by Rita Dove. Reprinted by permission of the author.

T. S. Eliot: *Rhapsody on a Windy Night; Aunt Helen;* and *The Hollow Men,* from COLLECTED POEMS, 1909–1962, by T. S. Eliot. Copyright 1936 by Harcourt, Inc. Copyright 1964, 1963 by T. S. Eliot. Reprinted by permission of Harcourt, Inc.

Martín Espada: *Bully* and *Jorge the Church Janitor Finally Quits,* from REBELLION IS THE CIRCLE OF A LOVER'S HANDS, by Martín Espada. Copyright 1990 by Martín Espada. Reprinted by permission of Curbstone Press. *The Lover of a Subversive Is Also a Subversive; Fidel in Ohio; Tires Stacked in the Hallways of Civilization; Who Burns for the Perfection of Paper;* and *The Music of Astronomy,* from CITY OF COUGHING AND DEAD RADIATORS, by Martín Espada. Copyright 1993 by Martín Espada. Reprinted by permission of W. W. Norton & Company, Inc.

Robert Frost: *Acquainted with the Night; Desert Places; The Subverted Flower;* and *Willful Homing,* from THE POETRY OF ROBERT FROST, by Robert Frost. Copyright 1928, 1969 by Henry Holt and Co. Copyright 1936, 1942, 1956 by Robert Frost. Copyright 1964, 1970 by Leslie Frost Ballantine. Reprinted by permission of Henry Holt and Company, LLC.

Allen Ginsberg: *Kaddish,* copyright 1959 by Allen Ginsberg; and *Fourth Floor, Dawn, Up All Night Writing Letters,* copyright 1982 by Allen Ginsberg, from COLLECTED POEMS, 1947–1980, by Allen Ginsberg. Reprinted by permission of HarperCollins Publishers, Inc. *Now and Forever,* from COSMOPOLITAN GREETINGS: POEMS, 1986–1992, by Allen Ginsberg. Copyright 1994 by Allen Ginsberg. Reprinted by permission of HarperCollins Publishers, Inc. *Homeless Compleynt* and *Peace in Bosnia-Herzegovina,* from DEATH AND FAME: LAST POEMS, 1993–1997, by Allen Ginsberg. Copyright 1999 by The Allen Ginsberg Trust. Reprinted by permission of HarperCollins Publishers, Inc.

Donald Hall: *My Son My Executioner; Digging; The Man in the Dead Machine; Woolworth's; Maple Syrup;* and *Kicking the Leaves,* from OLD AND NEW POEMS, by Donald Hall. Copyright 1990 by Donald Hall. Reprinted by permission of Houghton Mifflin Company. All rights reserved.

Michael S. Harper: *Letter to a Moon Child* and *Black Study,* from DEAR JOHN, DEAR COLTRANE, by Michael S. Harper. Copyright 1970 by Michael S. Harper. Reprinted by permission of the author. *The Dance of the Elephants,* from HISTORY IS YOUR OWN HEARTBEAT, by Michael S. Harper. Copyright 1971 by Michael S. Harper. Reprinted by permission of the author. *We Assume: On the Death of Our Son, Reuben Masai Harper,* by Michael S. Harper. Copyright 1968 by Michael S. Harper. Reprinted by permission of the author. *If You Don't Force It,* from THE AMERICAN SCHOLAR, by Michael S. Harper. Copyright 2000 by Michael S. Harper. Reprinted by permission of the author. *Release: Kind of Blue,* from SONGLINES IN MICHAELTREE, by Michael S. Harper. Copyright 2000 by Michael S. Harper. Reprinted by permission of the author.

Robert Hayden: *Belsen, Day of Liberation,* copyright 1985 by Emma Hayden; *Those Winter Sundays,* copyright 1966 by Robert Hayden; *For a Young Artist,* copyright 1985 by Emma Hayden; and *The Islands,* copyright 1978 by Robert Hayden, from COLLECTED POEMS OF ROBERT HAYDEN, by Robert Hayden, edited by Frederick Glaysher. Reprinted by permission of Liveright Publishing Corporation.

Jane Hirshfield: *For What Binds Us; Pomegranates; The Love of Aged Horses; The Weighing; Not Moving Even One Step; Standing Deer; Hope and Love;* and *Mathematics,* from OF GRAVITY AND ANGELS, by Jane Hirshfield. Copyright 1988 by Jane Hirshfield. Reprinted by permission of Wesleyan University Press.

Linda Hogan: *Nothing; Two of Hearts; Two; The New Apartment: Minneapolis;* and *Celebration: Birth of a Colt,* from THE BOOK OF MEDICINES, by Linda Hogan. Copyright 1993 by Linda Hogan. Reprinted by permission of Coffee House Press.

Langston Hughes: *The Negro Speaks of Rivers; I, Too; The Weary Blues; Railroad Avenue; Harlem Night; Theme for English B;* and *Harlem [2],* from THE COLLECTED POEMS OF LANGSTON HUGHES, by Langston Hughes. Copyright 1994 by The Estate of Langston Hughes. Reprinted by permission of Alfred A. Knopf, a division of Random House, Inc.

Randall Jarrell: *90 North; The Death of the Ball Turret Gunner; When I Was Home Last Christmas . . . ; The Woman at the Washington Zoo;* and *The Player Piano,* from THE COMPLETE POEMS, by Randall Jarrell. Copyright 1969, renewed 1997 by Mary von S. Jarrell. Reprinted by permission of Farrar, Straus, and Giroux, LLC.

Donald Justice: *Time and the Weather; Men at Forty; The Tourist from Syracuse; The Telephone Number of the Muse;* and *Poem,* from NEW AND SELECTED POEMS, by Donald Justice. Copyright 1995 by Donald Justice. Reprinted by permission of Alfred A. Knopf, a division of Random House, Inc. *The Missing Person,* from NIGHT LIGHT, by Donald Justice. Copyright 1967 by Donald Justice. Reprinted by permission of Wesleyan University Press.

Yusef Komunyakaa: *Out There There Be Dragons* and *Strands,* from THIEVES OF PARADISE, by Yusef Komunyakaa. Copyright 1998 by Yusef Komunyakaa. Reprinted by permission of Wesleyan University Press. *Untitled Blues* and *Villon/Leadbelly,* from COPACETIC, by Yusef Komunyakaa. Copyright 1984 by Yusef Komunyakaa. Reprinted by permission of Wesleyan University Press. *The Music That Hurts,* from I APOLOGIZE FOR THE EYES IN MY HEAD, by Yusef Komunyakaa. Copyright 1986 by Yusef Komunyakaa. Reprinted by permission of Wesleyan University Press. *Birds on a Powerline,* from NEON VERNACULAR, by Yusef Komunyakaa. Copyright 1993 by Yusef Komunyakaa. Reprinted by permission of Wesleyan University Press.

Maxine Kumin: *Morning Swim,* copyright 1965 by Maxine Kumin; *After Love,* copyright 1996 by Maxine Kumin; *Living Alone with Jesus,* copyright 1978 by Maxine Kumin; *The Longing to Be Saved,* copyright 1978 by Maxine Kumin; and *How It Is,* copyright 1978 by Maxine Kumin, from SELECTED POEMS, 1960–1990, by Maxine Kumin. Copyright 1996 by Maxine Kumin. Reprinted by permission of W. W. Norton & Company, Inc.

Li-Young Lee: *The Gift; Early in the Morning; Eating Alone;* and *Eating Together,* from ROSE, by Li-Young Lee. Copyright 1986 by Li-Young Lee. Reprinted by permission of BOA Editions, Ltd. *This Room and Everything in It* and *This Hour and What Is Dead,* from THE CITY IN WHICH I LOVE YOU, by Li-Young Lee. Copyright 1990 by Li-Young Lee. Reprinted by permission of BOA Editions, Ltd.

Denise Levertov: *The Lovers,* from COLLECTED EARLIER POEMS, 1940–1960, by Denise Levertov. Copyright 1946, 1957, 1958 by Denise Levertov. Reprinted by permission of New Directions Publishing Corporation. *A Woman Meets an Old Lover,* from POEMS, 1972–1982, by Denise Levertov. Copyright 1972, 1973, 1974, 1975, 1976, 1977, 1978, 1979, 1981, 1982 by Denise Levertov. Reprinted by permission of New Directions Publishing Corporation. *Wedding-Ring,* from LIFE IN THE FOREST, by Denise Levertov. Copyright 1978 by Denise Levertov. Reprinted by permission of New Directions Publishing Corporation. *Mid-American Tragedy* and *The Batterers,* from EVENING TRAIN, by Denise Levertov. Copyright 1992 by Denise Levertov. Reprinted by permission of New Directions Publishing Corporation.

John Logan: *Lines on His Birthday; Poem, Slow to Come, on the Death of Cummings (1894–1962); Poem for My Brother;* and *Believe It,* from JOHN LOGAN: THE COLLECTED POEMS, by John Logan. Copyright 1989 by the John Logan Literary Estate, Inc. Reprinted by permission of BOA Editions, Ltd.

Edgar Lee Masters: *"Butch" Weldy; Petit, the Poet; Anne Rutledge;* and *Lucinda Matlock,* from SPOON RIVER ANTHOLOGY, by Edgar Lee Masters. Reprinted by permission of Hilary Masters.

Naomi Shihab Nye: *Minnows; My Father and the Figtree; You Know Who You Are; What People Do;* and *Blood,* from WORDS UNDER THE WORDS: SELECTED POEMS, by Naomi Shihab Nye. Copyright 1995 by Naomi Shihab Nye. Reprinted by permission of Far Corner Books. *How Palestinians Keep Warm,* from RED SUITCASE, by Naomi Shihab Nye. Copyright 1994 by Naomi Shihab Nye. Reprinted by permission of BOA Editions, Ltd.

Frank O'Hara: *Why I Am Not a Painter; A True Account of Talking to the Sun at Fire Island; Pearl Harbor; For Grace, After a Party; To My Dead Father; Interior (with Jane);* and *Autobiographia Literaria,* from COLLECTED POEMS, by Frank O'Hara. Copyright 1971 by Maureen Granville-Smith, Administratrix of the Estate of Frank O'Hara. Reprinted by permission of Alfred A. Knopf, a division of Random House, Inc. *The Day Lady Died,* from LUNCH POEMS, by Frank O'Hara. Copyright 1964 by Frank O'Hara. Reprinted by permission of City Lights Books.

Marge Piercy: *For the young who want to; Sign; The skyscrapers of the financial district dance with Gasman; September afternoon at four o'clock;* and *Barbie doll,* from CIRCLES ON THE WATER, by Marge Piercy. Copyright 1982 by Marge Piercy. Reprinted by permission of Alfred A. Knopf, a division of Random House, Inc.

Sylvia Plath: *The Colossus,* from THE COLOSSUS AND OTHER POEMS, by Sylvia Plath. Copyright 1962 by Sylvia Plath. Reprinted by permission of Alfred A. Knopf, a division of Random House, Inc. *Mirror,* from CROSSING THE WATER, by Sylvia Plath. Copyright 1963 by Ted Hughes. Reprinted by permission of HarperCollins Publishers, Inc. *Lady Lazarus,* copyright 1963 by Ted Hughes; *Sheep in Fog,* copyright 1965 by Ted Hughes; and *Edge,* copyright 1963 by Ted Hughes, from ARIEL, by Sylvia Plath. Reprinted by permission of HarperCollins Publishers, Inc.

William Stafford: *Traveling Through the Dark; Notice What This Poem Is Not Doing;* and *American Gothic,* from THE WAY IT IS: NEW AND SELECTED POEMS, by William Stafford. Copyright 1998 by The Estate of William Stafford. Reprinted by permission of Graywolf Press. *Why I Am a Poet,* from MY NAME IS WILLIAM TELL, by William Stafford. Copyright 1992 by William Stafford. Reprinted by permission of Confluence Press. *What Gets Away,* from EVEN IN QUIET PLACES, by William Stafford. Copyright 1996 by The Estate of William Stafford. Reprinted by permission of Confluence Press.

Wallace Stevens: *From the Misery of Don Joost; Anecdote of the Jar; Frogs Eat Butterflies. Snakes Eat Frogs. Hogs Eat Snakes. Men Eat Hogs; Thirteen Ways of Looking at a Blackbird; How to Live. What to Do; The Poems of Our Climate; Study of Two Pears; The Idea of Order at Key West;* and *Of Mere Being,* from THE COLLECTED POEMS OF WALLACE STEVENS, by Wallace Stevens. Copyright 1954 by Wallace Stevens. Reprinted by permission of Alfred A. Knopf, a division of Random House, Inc.

Mark Strand: *Keeping Things Whole; Eating Poetry;* and *For Jessica, My Daughter,* from SELECTED POEMS, by Mark Strand. Copyright 1979, 1980 by Mark Strand. Reprinted by permission of Alfred A. Knopf, a division of Random House, Inc. *The Continuous Life* and *The End,* from THE CONTINUOUS LIFE, by Mark Strand. Copyright 1990 by Mark Strand. Reprinted by permission of Alfred A. Knopf, a division of Random House, Inc. *The Night, The Porch,* from BLIZZARD OF ONE, by Mark Strand. Copyright 1998 by Mark Strand. Reprinted by permission of Alfred A. Knopf, a division of Random House, Inc.

William Carlos Williams: *To Waken an Old Lady; The Young Housewife; Queen Anne's Lace; The Widow's Lament in Springtime; Spring and All; The Great Figure; This Is Just to Say; The Last Words of My English Grandmother; Landscape with the Fall of Icarus;* and *The Descent,* from COLLECTED POEMS, VOLUME 2: 1939–1962, by William Carlos Williams. Copyright 1948, 1962 by William Carlos Williams. Reprinted by permission of New Directions Publishing Corporation. *The Red Wheelbarrow* from COLLECTED POEMS, VOLUME 1: 1909–1939, by William Carlos Williams. Copyright 1938 by New Directions Publishing Corporation. Reprinted by permission of New Directions Publishing Corporation.

James Wright: *Saint Judas; Autumn Begins in Martins Ferry, Ohio; Lying in a Hammock at William Duffy's Farm in Pine Island, Minnesota; Beginning; Having Lost My Sons, I Confront the Wreckage of the Moon: Christmas, 1960;* and *A Prayer to Escape from the Market Place,* from ABOVE THE RIVER: THE COMPLETE POEMS, by James Wright. Copyright 1990 by Anne Wright. Reprinted by permission of Wesleyan University Press.

Ray A. Young Bear: *From the Spotted Night;* and *Wadaska Nakamoon, Vietnam Memorial,* from THE INVISIBLE MUSICIAN, by Ray A. Young Bear. Copyright 1990 by Ray A. Young Bear. Reprinted by permission of Holy Cow! Press. *Our Bird Aegis* and *The Mask of Four Indistinguishable Thunderstorms,* from THE ROCK ISLAND HIKING CLUB, by Ray A. Young Bear. Copyright 1996 by Ray A. Young Bear. Reprinted by permission of the University of Iowa Press.

Modern American Poetry

Book and cover design by William Seabright & Associates, Glencoe, Illinois.

Cover illustration is an untitled monotype by Sam Francis,
reproduced with permission from The Sam Francis Estate, Los Angeles,
copyright 2002.

Text set in Vendetta with Dalliance ornaments, both distributed by Emigre, Inc.,
and the Meta font family from FontFont.

Printed and bound by Malloy Lithographing in Ann Arbor, Michigan,
on 70# Finch Opaque.